VIEWPOINT

WORKBOOK

MICHAEL MCCARTHY
JEANNE MCCARTEN
HELEN SANDIFORD

CAMBRIDGE
UNIVERSITY PRESS

University Printing House, Cambridge CB2 8BS, United Kingdom

One Liberty Plaza, 20th Floor, New York, NY 10006, USA

477 Williamstown Road, Port Melbourne, VIC 3207, Australia

314–321, 3rd Floor, Plot 3, Splendor Forum, Jasola District Centre, New Delhi – 110025, India

79 Anson Road, #06–04/06, Singapore 079906

Cambridge University Press is part of the University of Cambridge.

It furthers the University's mission by disseminating knowledge in the pursuit of education, learning and research at the highest international levels of excellence.

www.cambridge.org
Information on this title: www.cambridge.org/9781107602779

First published 2012

20 19

Printed in Malaysia by Vivar Printing

A catalogue record for this publication is available from the British Library

ISBN 978-0-521-13186-5 Student's Book 1
ISBN 978-1-107-60151-2 Student's Book 1A
ISBN 978-1-107-60152-9 Student's Book 1B
ISBN 978-1-107-60277-9 Workbook 1
ISBN 978-1-107-60278-6 Workbook 1A
ISBN 978-1-107-60279-3 Workbook 1B
ISBN 978-1-107-60153-6 Teacher's Edition 1
ISBN 978-1-107-63988-1 Classroom Audio 1
ISBN 978-1-107-62978-3 Classware 1

Cover and interior design: Page 2, LLC
Layout/design services and photo research: Cenveo Publisher Services/Nesbitt Graphics, Inc.
Audio production: New York Audio Productions

Contents

Unit 1

Social networks

Lesson A Grammar Asking questions

A Complete the conversations with a correct form of the verbs given.

1. *A* Have you ever heard (hear) of speed-friending?
   B No, I haven't. What ____________ (be) it?
   A Well, it's a bit like speed-dating, but it's just a way of meeting people.
   B Interesting. So, ____________ you ever ____________ (go) to a speed-friending event?
   A No. But I'm thinking of going to one. ____________ you ____________ (want) to go with me?
   B Um, no, thanks. But tell me how it goes!

2. *A* ____________ I ____________ (tell) you I went to a networking event last week?
   B No. What kind of networking event ____________ (be) it?
   A It was for people who are looking for internships.
   B Oh, so ____________ you ____________ (look for) an internship right now?
   A Yeah. I'm trying to find one for the summer.
   B So ____________ you ____________ (make) any contacts at the event?
   A Yeah, actually, I did. I met some people from a software company.

About you

B Unscramble the questions. Then write answers that are true for you.

1. these days? / with / you / hanging out / are / Who
   Q: ______________________ A: ______________________
2. alone? / ever / Have / a weekend / spent / you
   Q: ______________________ A: ______________________
3. any of / you / call / Did / this morning? / your friends
   Q: ______________________ A: ______________________
4. in / Where / to / meet / you / people / go / your neighborhood? / can
   Q: ______________________ A: ______________________
5. your friends / you / all the time? / Do / text
   Q: ______________________ A: ______________________
6. outgoing / a kid? / Were / you / were / when / you
   Q: ______________________ A: ______________________
7. all your friends / joined / a social networking site? / Have
   Q: ______________________ A: ______________________
8. was / What / name / when / your / were / a kid? / best friend's / you
   Q: ______________________ A: ______________________

Lesson A Vocabulary Describing personality

A Complete the chart with the personality traits in the box.

aggressive	eccentric	narrow-minded	pushy	sensitive	thoughtful
annoying	intelligent	open-minded	relaxed	sweet	touchy
arrogant	laid-back	a pain	self-confident	talkative	weird

Generally positive	Generally negative	It depends . . .

B Complete the sentences with the words and expressions in Exercise A. Sometimes more than one option may be possible.

1. My boyfriend buys me flowers to say "thank you" and sends me cards to wish me luck. Yeah, he's very ______________ and ______________ .
2. My best friend's really smart. I mean, she's probably the most ______________ person I know.
3. Most people love my uncle. He's very ______________ . He'll chat to anybody about anything.
4. My brother was ______________ as a child. He was always getting into trouble for pushing other kids on the playground.
5. One of my best friends can seem a bit ______________ , like she thinks she's better than everybody else. I guess she's just ______________ – you know, she's pretty sure of herself.
6. My girlfriend gets upset easily. She's pretty ______________ .
7. My best friend never gets stressed about anything – you know, she's always ______________ , even before exams.
8. My mom's the kind of person who's always willing to listen to other people's ideas – you know, she's really ______________ .
9. One of my cousins is always bothering me. She's ______________ and very ______________ .
10. My neighbor has some very strong views and won't accept other people's opinions. He's so ______________ !

About you

C Complete the sentences to make them true for you. Use the words and expressions in Exercise A, and any other expressions you know.

1. I can't stand people who are ______________________________ .
2. If you want to be successful in business, you need to be ______________________ .
3. If you want to get along with people in general, you need to be ______________________ .
4. I really don't see myself as a/an ______________________________ person.
5. I like to think of myself as ______________ and ______________ .
6. One of my best friends is so ______________ and ______________ .
7. I usually choose ______________ and ______________ people as friends.
8. I don't mind people who are ______________ as long as they're ______________ , too.

Lesson B Grammar Talking about habits

A Complete the sentences with a correct form of the verbs given.

1. My best friend can be really annoying. She __________ constantly __________ (look) at her phone. When we __________ (watch) a movie, she checks her email all the time. And when we're out together, she __________ always __________ (take) pictures of stuff. Then she __________ (post) the photos online. I mean, I'm usually pretty laid-back, but it's starting to drive me crazy.
2. My sister and I are actually really close, but we __________ (not call) each other very often. Occasionally we __________ (will / text) pictures to each other – or email stuff. But we're both so busy, we __________ (not answer) each other's emails unless it's really important. When she __________ (call), we __________ (talk) for hours.
3. I __________ (not waste) a lot of time online. You know, I __________ probably __________ (will / surf) the Internet for a couple of hours a day. But not all at once. I __________ (tend / take) about half an hour before work and probably half an hour at lunchtime to look at stuff online. And I __________ (email) people at night. But a lot of my friends __________ (will / stay) online for hours and hours.

B Circle the best option to complete the conversations.

1. *A* How many times a day do you text your friends?
   B Well, **I'll send / I'm sending** a reply whenever I get a message. So, I don't know – maybe 20 or 30 times a day. Mostly, **we make / we're making** plans by text. But **I tend to call / I'm calling** if I want to have a real conversation or something.
2. *A* How do you keep in touch with your family when you're away from home?
   B When **I'll travel / I'm traveling**, we try to video-chat on the Internet. That way we can talk for free. And **we'll email / we're emailing**, too. I like to keep in touch.
3. *A* Have you ever used the Internet to find a friend?
   B Yeah. **I'm searching / I'm always searching** online to see if I can find my old school friends. **I'll find / I'm finding** someone every once in a while. It's fun to see what they're doing now. Occasionally **I'll contact / I'm contacting** them. But **I don't do / I'm not doing** it often.

About you

C Now write your own answers to the questions in Exercise B.

1. ______________________________

   ____
2. ______________________________

   ____
3. ______________________________

   ____

Lesson C Conversation strategies

A Read the conversations. Circle the appropriate follow-up questions.

1. *A* How do you usually keep in touch with your friends back home?
   B How do we keep in touch? We tend to text. Or we'll check each other's profile pages.
   A **And do you ever call each other? / And you never keep in touch with them?**
   B Yeah. Sometimes.

2. *A* So, yeah, Mark and I have been dating for ten months now.
   B That's great. **But you lost touch, right? / So, you're getting along well?**
   A Yeah. It's great. He's so thoughtful and just a really cool guy.

3. *A* My parents got divorced when I was little.
   B That's too bad. That must have been hard.
   A Yeah, but my mom remarried, and my stepdad's great. He's really cool.
   B That's good. **But you don't see your mom, right? / So you do a lot together?**
   A Yeah. We always hang out as a family.

B Read the conversations. Write the appropriate follow-up question for each conversation. There are two extra questions.

a. And does he know you at all?	d. But you wouldn't tell them, right?
b. And how often do you see them?	e. So you didn't talk to each other at all?
c. But would you feel sad?	

1. *A* How would you feel if you lost touch with a good friend?
   B It depends. It happens sometimes.
   A ______________________________
   B I guess so. Again, it depends.

2. *A* Have you ever had a fight with a friend over something silly?
   B Yeah, once. My friend Jack and I had an argument about this girl. We didn't speak for weeks.
   A ______________________________
   B No, not a word.

3. *A* Have you always had a lot of friends or just one or two close friends?
   B I tend to have one or two close friends. I don't have a big circle of friends.
   A ______________________________
   B Oh, we hang out pretty often, like once or twice during the week and then every weekend.

Lesson D **Reading** Personal profiles

A Prepare Circle two facts and underline three pieces of advice. Who is this information for – employers or candidates?

Getting the most from online profiles

1 Over 30 percent of employers say they currently use, or plan to use, social networking sites to obtain information about job candidates. However, only 16 percent of workers write their online profiles with potential employers in mind.

2 What may be more worrying for today's job seekers is that 34 percent of managers said they have rejected a candidate because of the information they obtained online. Finding inappropriate photographs is one of the main reasons for rejection.

3 This trend of using social networking sites as an employment tool is growing. "We can learn a lot about a candidate from his or her online profile," says Mindy Watson, director of human resources at an advertising agency. "We want to see if the person will fit in well at our company, so the information in an online profile is valuable to us."

4 Hiring managers also tend to use social networking sites when they are looking for new hires. So if you want to use your profile to find a new job either now or in the future, here are some do's and don'ts.

5 ➤ ☐ Keep your profile up to date, even if you are not looking for a job. Make sure you list your latest achievements. Hiring managers are looking for the best people for their companies, so make sure that you present yourself in a positive way. You never know – someone may invite you to come in for an interview even before you start looking for a new job.

6 ➤ ☐ It is always best to avoid making any negative comments about your current or previous boss, company, or co-workers. If employers think that you will damage their image after you leave the company, they won't want to hire you.

7 ➤ ☐ If you are always telling off-color jokes or joining weird or silly groups, be careful. One of the fun things about networking sites is that you can connect with other people who share your sense of humor. However, these groups don't always leave a potential employer with a good impression. Instead, be selective and join groups that demonstrate your professional goals or social involvement. This shows you are thoughtful and creates a positive online image.

8 ➤ ☐ Be careful also if you are trying to hide your job search from your current boss. One of your co-workers might see your profile and mention it. You could find that your boss withholds that promotion or raise you were expecting. However, if your boss does find out and accuses you of looking for a new job, don't deny it. It is better to tell the truth than risk a negative reference.

9 ➤ ☐ Remember that other people will see the contacts you have made if you don't keep your friends list private. So in addition to keeping your friends' inappropriate pictures and comments off your profile, be cautious about who your online friends are.

10 ➤ ☐ Review the pictures you have uploaded to your profile, the personal information you have given, and any blogs or sites you have linked to. Delete anything you might regret later.

11 Always bear in mind that employers can use your social networking profile to evaluate you, so show self-confidence (without being arrogant) and promote yourself well. Think of it as a face-to-face meeting with an employer, and present the image of yourself that you want to promote.

B Information flow **Where do these headings fit in the article? Write the letters a–f in the boxes in the article.**

a. Don't badmouth your current or previous employer
b. Don't forget: Others can see your friends
c. Don't mention your job search if you are still employed
d. Do join groups . . . selectively
e. Do update your profile regularly
f. Do clean up your "digital dirt"

C Read for detail **Are the sentences true or false, or is the information not given in the article? Write T, F, or NG. Correct the false sentences.**

1. Companies use social networking sites to obtain information about their employees' family life. ____
2. Your online profile can get you a job, even if you're not looking for one. ____
3. It's a good idea to show your sense of humor in your profile. ____
4. If your boss finds out about your job search, you should deny it. ____
5. You can get fired from your current job because of your online profile. ____
6. When you're looking for a job, it matters who your online friends are. ____
7. It's fine to be arrogant in your profile, if you're promoting yourself. ____
8. When you write a profile, you should imagine you're talking to an employer. ____

D Focus on vocabulary **Replace the words in bold with the verbs and expressions from the article.**

1. Employers ~~**get**~~ obtain information about candidates from their online profiles. (para. 1)
2. One reason employers have **not hired** candidates is because of inappropriate photos. (para. 2)
3. Your boss might **not give you** a promotion if he or she knows you are looking for a job. (para. 8)
4. If your boss **says you're** looking for another job, don't **say you aren't doing** it. (para. 8)
5. Don't post anything you'll **be sorry about** later. (para. 10)
6. The best way to **show people your good qualities** is to have a clean profile. (para. 11)

E **Write a response to each of the sentences in Exercise D. Use the verbs and expressions from the article.**

1. I think this happens all the time. When I applied for a job, they obtained information about me from my online profile.
2. ____
3. ____
4. ____
5. ____
6. ____

Writing A script for an online debate

A **Read the debate script. Circle the correct words to show contrasting ideas.**

Social networks – a waste of time or a good way to find a job?

Some people believe that social networks are a waste of time. **However, / On the one hand,** other people enjoy using them to keep in touch with friends and family. **While / On the one hand,** it is fun to have an online profile and share news and photographs with people you know. **On the other hand, / Whereas** it is important to realize that employers can use your profile to see if they want to hire you. **While / However,** you might think your pictures are harmless, employers might not agree. If you have a profile on a social networking site, make sure you promote a professional image. In conclusion, it is better to keep your profile up to date with appropriate content, or it might cost you your dream job.

Help note: ***Contrasting ideas***

However, and ***On the other hand,*** contrast the ideas in a previous sentence with the ideas in a new sentence.

While and ***whereas*** contrast ideas within one sentence.

In sentences with ***while*** and ***whereas***, use a comma at the end of the first clause.

B Editing **Read the Help note. Then correct the mistakes in these extracts from scripts. Change the expression, or the punctuation, or both. There is more than one correct answer.**

1. You might think your party photos are harmless. **Whereas** employers might see them in a different way. You might think your party photos are harmless. However, employers might see them in a different way.
2. Some people never put photos on their profiles **on the other hand** other people post a lot of pictures. ______
3. Job seekers are not cleaning up their profiles **however** employers are checking them. ______
4. **However** an online profile may be public, it is not fair to use it to reject a job candidate. ______
5. **While** I understand why employers check people's profiles online. Personal profiles are not meant for employers. ______
6. You can control who sees your résumé **however** you can't always control who has access to your online profile. ______

C **Write a script for the debate in Exercise A. Include an introduction, contrasting ideas, and a conclusion. Then check your script for errors.**

These days everyone uses social networking sites, and job seekers are using them to promote themselves to potential employers. While you might think your personal profile is private, . . .

Listening extra Keeping in touch

A Check (✓) the expressions that describe ending relationships.

- ☐ break up with
- ☐ fall out with
- ☐ get divorced
- ☐ get engaged
- ☐ get married
- ☐ lose touch with
- ☐ make friends
- ☐ separate
- ☐ "unfriend"

B Listen to four people talk about relationships. Answer the questions. Write the names. There is one extra question.

Andrea Nuray Oscar Christa

1. Who would never contact someone from a previous relationship? ____________
2. Who "unfriends" people occasionally? ____________
3. Who is getting divorced soon? ____________
4. Who lost touch with someone over a period of time? ____________
5. Who just got back in touch with someone after a long time? ____________

C Listen again. Are the sentences true or false? Write T or F. Correct the false sentences.

Andrea

1. Andrea and her roommate stopped calling because they had an argument. ____
2. They only keep in touch on special occasions. ____

Nuray

3. Nuray likes to know what her old friends are doing every day. ____
4. Sometimes she'll contact her old boyfriends online. ____

Oscar

5. Oscar has too many friends to keep in touch with. ____
6. He gets upset when he reads mean comments on his profile. ____

Christa

7. Christa's life has changed a lot in the last ten years. ____
8. She finds it difficult to keep in touch with her husband when she's traveling. ____

D Listen again to the last thing each person says. Do you agree or disagree? Write a sentence expressing your views.

1. ____
2. ____
3. ____
4. ____

Now complete the *Unit 1 Progress chart* on page 98.

Unit 2

The media

Lesson A Grammar Adding information

A Is the information in bold essential, or is it extra? Write D (defining, or essential) or N (non-defining, or extra). Then add commas where necessary.

1. I can't stand magazines **that are full of ads.** _____
2. Fashion magazines **which are really mostly about shopping** usually have the most ads. _____
3. The celebrities **who are always in the gossip magazines** don't really interest me. _____
4. Good theater actors **who never get as famous as movie actors** deserve more attention. _____
5. I really enjoy reading about celebrities and the charity work **they do.** _____
6. When I buy music magazines, I'll usually buy the ones **which have a free CD.** _____
7. The magazine **I like the most** is about art and culture. _____

B Complete the conversations with *who, that,* or *which.* If you can leave them out, write parentheses ( ) around them. Sometimes there is more than one correct answer.

1. *A* I'm looking for a good TV show _________ could help me improve my listening skills in English. What do you think I should watch?
   B I think maybe sitcoms, _________ are often about everyday life, are best for that. Check out the two _________ I watch – Wednesday nights at 8:00 and 8:30 on Channel 2.
2. *A* Look at this magazine _________ I just bought . . . it's full of ads! Why can't I find magazines _________ aren't trying to sell me stuff?
   B Well, magazines have to make money, _________ ads provide.
3. *A* Ugh, I can't listen to any more about that actress, Leya March, _________ seems to be on the news every minute of the day!
   B Oh, I find it all pretty entertaining. And most of the events _________ are happening in the world are pretty depressing, so hearing about her is kind of a relief.
4. *A* I'm obsessed with reality shows. The people _________ are on them are hilarious.
   B I know. They'll do anything to be famous, _________ can be so funny to watch.

C Complete the sentences with relative clauses using *who, that,* or *which* and the information in parentheses. Add commas where necessary.

1. The TV show ______________ is about a group of college students. (I like it best of all.)
2. My best friend ______________ has a TV in every room. (She watches TV constantly.)
3. The online magazine ______________ is about current events. (I read it the most.)
4. I watch TV every night to relax ______________. (I need to do that before I go to bed.)
5. Some people are obsessed with celebrity gossip ______________. (I think it's ridiculous.)

Lesson B Vocabulary Describing research

A Circle the correct prepositions to complete the sentences.

1. There is a lot of concern **about / on / of** violence on TV.
2. Research has shown that exposure to violent TV shows has an effect **to / on / with** the brain.
3. One reason **for / between / of** lower test scores is that kids spend more time on the Internet.
4. We don't know enough about the impact of TV **in / on / with** the youngest children.
5. Many of the ads on TV **between / on / for** junk food are aimed at children.
6. The rise **in / on / with** Internet advertising may affect young people's habits, too.
7. Scientists don't know all the causes **of / with / about** obesity in young people.
8. There may be a relationship **on / with / between** watching TV and language development.

B Complete the blog post with the words in the box. Sometimes more than one answer is possible.

concern	impact	increase	influence	link	✔ problem	research

Menu Home Channels Browse Settings

Is there a problem with TV?

Some researchers believe that watching TV has a huge ________ on children. Some experts claim that they have found a ________ between watching TV and learning problems in children. However, people don't have the same ________ about educational TV shows. It's my feeling that we should look at their ________ on children, too. While it's likely that some educational shows are good for children, what's disturbing is that there has been a large ________ in advertising for fast food and other junk food during these programs. I believe these commercials contribute to unhealthy eating habits. So before I make a decision about TV for my kids, I need to know more. What I'm saying is, we need more ________ on this subject.

Posted by Blog Girl, March 3

About you

C Answer the questions with your own opinions.

1. Do you think watching TV has an impact on your own behavior? Why or why not?
   ____
2. Do you have any concerns about young children and TV?
   ____
3. Why do you think there is a relationship between watching TV and obesity in young people?
   ____
4. Do you think watching TV is the main cause of poor test results? Why or why not?
   ____

Lesson B Grammar Linking ideas

A Complete the information about TV viewing. Use *that* or the correct form of *be* + *that*.

How much TV do you watch every week? You may think ________ you watch too much TV. But what's surprising about today's TV shows ________ they might actually help your brain. It's probably true ________ many people watch shows with no real benefit. However, some experts now claim ________ TV shows today are more advanced than ever. One key difference ________ they have more complex stories. Experts claim ________ the brain has to work harder to understand them. So next time you want to watch TV, don't feel guilty! Go ahead and turn it on. It just might be making you smarter.

B Rewrite the sentences using a *that* clause. Start with the words given in parentheses, and add a verb where necessary.

1. TV and the Internet have changed children's reading habits. (Some experts . . .)
   Some experts agree that TV and the Internet have changed children's reading habits.
2. Many children prefer watching TV to reading. (What's clear . . .)
   ____
3. Reading improves children's vocabulary development. (One problem with spending less time reading . . .)
   ____
4. Most books and magazines will only be online in the future. (It's likely . . .)
   ____
5. Publishers may stop printing books altogether. (What's interesting . . .)
   ____
6. Going digital is inevitable. (Many people believe . . .)
   ____

About you

C Complete the sentences with your own ideas about the impact of TV and the Internet.

1. It's not surprising ________________________________.
2. Many people feel ________________________________.
3. What's clear is ________________________________.
4. It's possible ________________________________.
5. One problem with the Internet is ________________________________.
6. It's true ________________________________.

Lesson C Conversation strategies

A Complete the conversation with the *which* comments in the box. There is one extra.

which always ends up being expensive	which is so annoying
which is not surprising	which totally goes against what I just said

Marco I really hate getting junk email.

Lina Me, too. Like those email chains people send. There's one I've seen at least ten times.

Marco ________________________________.

Lina I know. Some of them are so stupid.

Marco Wait, though. Somebody sent me a video clip a couple of days ago. Hold on, you have to see this – ________________________________.

Lina Um, OK . . .

Marco Oh. They must have taken it off. It's not here anymore.

Lina ________________________________. Happens all the time – you finally find a good one, and it's gone.

B Complete the conversations with *You know what . . . ?* Use the information in parentheses.

1. *A* Video ads are all over the place. It's so annoying.
   B You know what really gets me? They're in your personal email. (It really gets me.)
2. *A* Check this out – do you know about this video site? It's awesome.
   B Yeah, it's great. And ________________________________ I'm totally addicted to it. (It's ridiculous.)
3. *A* My friend's constantly posting videos and pictures of me without asking.
   B ________________________________ When you start looking for a job, employers can see those pictures and videos. (I'd be concerned about this.)

C Complete the conversations with the expressions in the box.

just so annoying	I prefer	really bothers me
really scares me	so convenient	so important

1. *A* You know what ______________? You can't watch a video clip on this website without watching an ad first. And you can't skip it!
   B Which is ______________. There should be a way to get past it.
2. *A* Are you still watching DVDs on your laptop?
   B Yeah. I can take them with me when I travel, which is ______________.
   A It is. But you know what ______________? Just downloading them off the Internet.
3. *A* I finally figured out how to add privacy controls to my profile.
   B Which is ______________, especially now that you're looking for a job.
   A Yeah, but you know what ______________? My friends who *don't* use privacy controls.

Lesson D Reading Distractions

A **Prepare** **If something is *distracting,* it takes your attention away from what you're doing. Think of three distractions – things that you find distracting – in your daily life.**

B **Read for main ideas** **Read the article. Does the writer mention any of the distractions you thought of in Exercise A?**

DISTRACTIONS: Should we be concerned?

1 Young people have always been faced with distractions, but now with computers, video games, tablets, and smart phones, there are even more things demanding their attention. A recent study found that more than half of students – aged 8 to 18 – are distracted while doing homework, and for 56 percent of the time they are also using the Internet, watching TV, or using some other form of media. Should we be concerned about these kinds of distractions?

2 Some researchers say that one problem with these technologies is that they have a greater impact on young people. First, young people's brains become used to constantly switching tasks, which makes them less able to pay attention for long periods of time. Second, some experts say that distraction has an impact on people's ability to think deeply.

3 One study looked at the computer use of students in grades 5 through 8. The researchers found a link between access to home computers and a drop in reading and math scores. What is clear, they say, is that middle graders are mostly using computers to socialize and play games rather than for educational purposes. The study used data from 2000 to 2005, before the huge rise in social networking sites, so the problem may be even more extreme today.

4 In other studies, researchers have shown that boys who have access to video game systems at home are frequently distracted from their homework. The research showed that the boys' reading and writing scores suffered as a result. It's also possible that playing video games, which involves multitasking (doing more than one thing at a time) has more impact on the brain than distractions such as watching TV. In one study, boys aged 12 to 14 spent an hour every other night playing video games after they finished their homework. On the other evenings, they spent an hour watching a movie on TV. The researchers found that on nights when the boys watched TV, they slept better than when they played video games. The video games also had a negative impact on the boys' ability to remember vocabulary, even words that they were already familiar with.

5 What kinds of activities, then, should we encourage children to do? Some scientists say that reading books is a good choice because children are less distracted when they read books. This may be because children identify with the characters and are able to focus their attention for longer periods of time. Many studies have found that students who read books have significantly higher test scores than students who don't.

6 On the other hand, critics of these studies claim that playing complex computer games and doing Internet searches actually improve a person's ability to concentrate and stay focused. They say that books promote one type of learning, whereas the Internet promotes a different, equally beneficial type.

7 The impact of computer use on the brain is a complex issue, and not all experts agree on its positive and negative effects. What is clear is that electronic media are here to stay. For this reason, education experts may need to turn their attention to designing educational technology that helps students focus on learning and not be distracted by the media they are using.

C Understanding viewpoints **Check (✔) the points that the writer makes in the article.**

☐ 1. Many children are being distracted by electronic media while they are doing homework.

☐ 2. Some distractions can be more harmful than others.

☐ 3. Watching a movie has a more positive effect on the brain than doing activities that involve multitasking.

☐ 4. Children who read books do well in all of their school subjects.

☐ 5. Experts all agree that technology has negative effects.

D Read for detail **Circle the correct information to make true sentences about the article.**

1. According to the article, various technologies distract children because **young learners think they're fun / the user has to constantly switch tasks**.
2. The article suggests that **watching TV / playing video games** is a form of multitasking.
3. One study showed that **TV / video games** had a more negative impact on young boys' sleep.
4. This study also showed that **watching TV / playing video games** had an effect on the boys' ability to remember vocabulary.
5. The study in which researchers found a link between home computers and lower test scores used information from **before / after** the huge rise in social networking.
6. **Critics / Supporters** of these studies say playing video games and surfing the Internet actually improve people's ability to concentrate.
7. The writer suggests that educational researchers should be focusing on improving online materials because electronic media **are better than books / aren't going to disappear**.

E Focus on vocabulary **Find these words and expressions in the text. Match them with their meanings. Write the letters a–f.**

1. extreme (para. 3) ____	a. start looking at
2. be familiar with (para. 4) ____	b. people who don't like an idea
3. identify with (para. 5) ____	c. know
4. critics of (para. 6) ____	d. feel a connection with
5. a complex issue (para. 7) ____	e. a difficult subject
6. turn attention to (para. 7) ____	f. very great

F **Do you think that technology has a positive or negative impact on your ability to study? Give reasons for your answer.**

____

____

____

____

____

____

____

____

Writing A one-paragraph essay

Essay question

Should video websites warn teenagers about dangerous behavior?

A **Read the essay and the Help note. Underline the topic sentence. Then add the words in the box to the sentences with supporting details. Use commas where necessary.**

First	Second	Third	Finally

Video websites should warn teenagers about dangerous behavior for several reasons. Teenagers tend to take more risks because their brains are at a particular stage of development. With the rise in Internet video sites, teenagers can see people doing all kinds of dangerous activities, and some feel pressure to copy what they see. Some children are taking great risks and filming these activities so they can share the videos with their friends. The Internet makes sharing the videos easy – teens who want to impress their friends simply have to upload a clip to their profile page.

Help note: *Commas after listing expressions*

Use a comma after ***First***, ***Second***, ***Third***, ***Lastly***, and ***Finally***.

B Editing **Correct the errors in these sentences and add punctuation, where necessary. One sentence is correct.**

I don't agree that video websites should have warnings for teenagers. At first many teenagers are very responsible. Second it is not the Internet's responsibility if someone does something dangerous. Third parents should be responsible for their children's behavior. At last the reasons for dangerous behavior are not always clear.

C **Write a paragraph to answer the essay question. State your opinion in a clear topic sentence, and give at least three reasons to support it. Then check your paragraph for errors.**

___

___

___

___

___

___

___

___

___

Listening extra *Talk Tuesday*

A What words and expressions would you expect to hear in a debate about television and children? Add four more ideas to the chart.

get rid of TV	educational	a waste of time	fun
______	______	______	______

B Listen to the introduction to a radio call-in show. Check (✔) the correct answers to the questions.

1. What is the main topic of the show?
   - ☐ a. Should children watch TV and if so, what type?
   - ☐ b. Do children need a break from school work?
   - ☐ c. Why do children spend too much time watching TV?

2. What are some of the topics that parents are debating?
   - ☐ a. Should parents watch TV with their children?
   - ☐ b. Should children watch TV at all?
   - ☐ c. When should children watch TV?
   - ☐ d. Should all children's TV programs be educational?

C Listen to three callers to the radio show. Are the sentences true or false? Write T or F. Correct the false sentences.

Mike

Michiko

Angelo

1. Mike is concerned about all the advertisements on TV that target kids. ______
2. He got rid of his TV a few years ago. ______
3. He believes children should spend their time in more useful ways. ______
4. Michiko thinks parents are the best teachers. ______
5. She thinks TV can be educational. ______
6. She's worried about her children watching shows in Spanish. ______
7. Angelo believes that watching TV is a big issue. ______
8. He thinks it's important that parents decide what children watch on TV. ______
9. He thinks the main problem is that people who watch TV are less intelligent. ______

About you

D Listen again. Do you agree or disagree with the callers' opinions? Write one opinion that each caller gives, and complete the rest of the sentence with your own views.

1. Mike says that ______, which I think is ______.
2. Michiko believes that ______, and what's interesting is that ______.
3. Angelo thinks that ______, which is totally ______.

Now complete the *Unit 2 Progress chart* on page 98.

Unit 3

Stories

Lesson A Grammar Talking about the past

A Match the sentences with the correct timeline. Write a or b.

1. My English class has been so much more interesting since the winter break. b
2. When I was in high school, I studied in Mexico City for a semester. ____
3. I volunteered at a children's sports camp last summer. ____
4. Our teacher still hasn't given us our grades for the class project. ____
5. I've been taking violin lessons since elementary school. ____
6. My family moved to this neighborhood a few years ago. ____

a. past time now

b. past time ⟶ now

B Circle the best verb forms to complete the sentences.

1. **Have you learned / Did you learn** Chinese when you were in Kunming?
2. So far, I **haven't traveled / didn't travel** to any other continents besides Europe.
3. After I **was getting / got** my license, I **have driven / drove** across the U.S. with my sister.
4. I **haven't been enjoying / didn't enjoy** my cooking class lately. I hope it gets better soon.
5. My brother **has joined / joined** a book club, but he **was quitting / quit** after a few weeks.
6. I really **have enjoyed / enjoyed** my job at the park last summer. I**'ve been working / was working** on the trails.

C Complete the conversations with the verbs given. Use an appropriate past tense or present perfect form. Sometimes more than one option may be possible.

1. *A* I haven't seen you in months! What have you been doing lately?
   B Oh, a lot of stuff, actually. I've been working (work) on my apartment – you know, cleaning and painting. I ________ (start) a few weekends ago, and it already looks great. How about you? What ________ (go on) with you lately?
   A Well, for the last month, I ________ (volunteer) as a tutor. I help kids with their homework after school. I ________ (be) surprised at first – it's actually a lot of fun. And there's my softball team, too. So far, I ________ (not score) any runs, but I never miss a game!
2. *A* Have you ever had a life-changing experience?
   B Actually, yeah. One semester, I ________ (work) at a homeless shelter. It ________ (not be) easy, you know, seeing people in such difficult situations, but I really ________ (love) the work. At the time, I ________ (major) in math, but after that semester I ________ (change) my major to social work, which I ________ (study) ever since. I ________ (not decide) what I want to do when I graduate, but I know I want to help people.

D Write true sentences about something . . .

1. you haven't done recently. I haven't gone bowling in a long time. I miss it!
2. you were doing earlier this year. ________
3. you've been doing regularly. ________
4. you did last weekend. ________
5. you haven't done yet (but need to soon!). ________

Lesson B Vocabulary Expressions for school

A Match the words in bold with the expressions that have a similar meaning. Write a–f.

a. fall behind on	c. miss	e. affect my grades
b. struggle with	d. complete the questions	f. leave it blank

1. It's a timed test. You have to **finish it** in 20 minutes. ____
2. I get really stressed-out when **I'm late with** my work. ____
3. When I get a cold, I usually **don't go to** a lot of classes. ____
4. I really **have a difficult time doing** math. It's been a problem since high school. ____
5. If I can't answer a question on an exam, I usually **don't write anything** at first, and then I come back to it later. ____
6. I've been going out too much, and it's really starting to **have a negative impact on my schoolwork.** ____

B Complete the conversation with the verbs in the box. Use each verb only once.

affect	count toward	✔ finished	missed	turned . . . in
caught up on	fall behind on	left . . . blank	struggled with	

A Have you ___finished___ your take-home exam yet?
B Yes, I ____________ it ____________ yesterday. It was tough – I really ____________ it. What about you?
A I'm still having trouble. I've so much going on, and I'm starting to ____________ my work.
B Yeah? Hey, what did you think about the second question?
A The second question? . . . Oh, right. Impossible. For now, I've just ____________ it ____________.
B I know. I don't think I answered it very well. I know it'll ____________ my grade.
A How much does this test ____________ our final grade, anyway? Do you know?
B I have no idea. I ____________ the first class when the professor explained all that stuff.
A Well, I sure will be glad when I've ____________ my work. Then I'll be able to relax a little.

About you

C Answer the questions with information that is true for you.

1. What are two good reasons to miss a class?
____
2. What can you do when you fall behind on your work?
____
3. Do you think attendance should count toward your grade? Why or why not?
____
4. When do you think it's better to leave a question blank on a test?
____
5. What subjects or tasks do you sometimes struggle with?
____

Lesson B **Grammar** Sequencing events

A **Which event happened first (1)? Which happened next (2)? Write 1 or 2 in each box.**

1. I was nervous the day of the exam [2], even though I'd been studying for over a week [1].
2. A classmate had warned me about this professor's tests [ ], but I didn't believe him [ ].
3. So later on, I asked my physics teacher for help [ ]. I'd managed to stop her in the hall [ ].
4. I didn't do well on the exam [ ], even though I'd asked that teacher for help [ ].

B **Complete the conversations with the verbs given. Use the simple past, past perfect, or past perfect continuous. Sometimes there is more than one correct answer.**

1. *A* Had you ever lived (live) abroad before you ________ (move) here?
   B Yeah. One summer in grad school, I ________ (go) to Argentina and ________ (get) a job on a horse ranch.
   A Really? So have you been back to Argentina?
   B Yes! I ________ (go) back a few months ago. I ________ (think) about it for ages and finally ________ (decide) to go in August. I ________ (visit) my host family, who I ________ (not see) in years . . . and, of course, the horses!

2. *A* I haven't seen you in ages! What have you been up to?
   B Well, for one thing, I ________ (move) and ________ (change) jobs in April.
   A Wow, you left your cool publishing job? Why?
   B Well, things ________ (not go) well. I ________ (get) into an argument with my boss a few weeks before I ________ (quit), and things never really ________ (get) better.

3. *A* Why didn't you go to grad school?
   B Well, right before I ________ (graduate) from art school, I ________ (take) an entry-level job at a gallery. You know, I ________ (be) a little scared because I ________ (not earn) any money in a while. I ________ (hope) to go to grad school, but I ________ (need) money. So one day, I ________ (run) into a family friend that I ________ (not see) in a long time. When she found out I was an art major, she ________ (offer) me a job. And with the connections I've made, I'm actually selling some of my own paintings now!

C **Read the situations and complete the sentences with a correct form of the verbs given.**

1. I was waiting for my friends. An hour later, they finally showed up.
   When my friends finally ________ , I ________ for them for an hour. (show up / wait)
2. I called my advisor a few times last week. He never called back. I finally got an email from him yesterday.
   Yesterday I finally ________ an email from my advisor. I ________ him a few times last week, but he ________ . (get / call / not call back)
3. I cleaned my apartment last night. Then I did my homework. Then I watched TV.
   Last night I ________ my apartment, ________ my homework, and ________ TV. (clean / do / watch)
4. Last week our teacher reminded us to study the new vocabulary. On Monday he gave us a test. I was surprised.
   Our teacher ________ us a test on Monday. At first I was surprised, but then I remembered he ________ us to study last Friday. (give / remind)

Lesson C Conversation strategies

A Read the conversation. Circle the sentences when Jen interrupts her story, and underline the sentences when she comes back to it.

Jen Remember Mr. Jopling, our old history teacher? I ran into him yesterday.

Kim Really? Wow. Of course I remember him.

Jen Yeah, so I was in line right behind him. When I think about it, I just feel so ashamed. We were so awful to him.

Kim I know. It's embarrassing.

Jen So anyway, I saw him in line at the movies. He recognized me, and he even remembered my name. Twenty-five years later! Can you believe that? Looking back, I guess we probably made a pretty strong impression. We were constantly – I mean, constantly – passing notes back and forth. So yeah, where was I? Oh! So he told me he actually still has one of our notes.

Kim What? No way!

Jen Yeah. Get this. It's on his desk, in a frame. It says, in my handwriting, "I am sooooo bored." When I think about it, I just want to crawl under a rock. But anyway, you know what he told me? He told me that because of that note, he always tries hard to make his classes interesting.

Kim That's unbelievable. I mean, that's totally crazy.

B Match the sentences and the responses. Write the letters a–d.

1. When we were kids, my parents used to make us listen to opera every Sunday. ____
2. When I was little, I used to make clothes for all my dolls. ____
3. I love looking at old family pictures. ____
4. When I was a kid, I used to hang out in the kitchen as my grandmother prepared incredible meals. She was amazing! ____

a. Well, no wonder you hate it now!
b. No wonder you're such a good cook!
c. It's no wonder you became a fashion designer.
d. No wonder. They probably bring back great memories.

C Complete the anecdote with the expressions in the box. Write the letters a–e.

a. anyway b. It's no wonder c. Looking back d. when I think about it e. Where was I

"You know what I regret? I lost touch with my best friend from high school after we had a big fight. One day he told me about a personal problem and asked me not to tell anyone. I really wanted to help him, you know? But ____ , I was so young . . . I didn't know how to help. ____ ? Oh, right. So I asked another friend what she would do in my friend's situation. I didn't say his name, but she guessed who it was. ____ , I guess I thought I could trust her. I'll never make a mistake like that again, you know, telling someone else's secrets. So ____ , she told my best friend she knew about his problem. He was really embarrassed. ____ he hasn't spoken to me since."

Lesson D Reading A short story

A React Read the short story. Does it have a happy ending? Why or why not?

Lion

1 When he was a small child, Lucas charged around the house like a lion. He roared, jumped out from behind the couch, slapped his tiny lion paws down on the table, and scared his baby sister. "Stop that!" his mother yelled, tugging his shirt hard. "You are not a lion. You are a little boy! Start acting like one!" Because he was not actually a lion, he thought maybe he could be a superhero. "But what do you really want to be?" his grandfather asked him one day as he slipped a dish of ice cream across the kitchen table. He wanted to be a police officer – or maybe a soldier or a firefighter. He wanted to be something big and strong, like a lion.

2 When Lucas was starting high school, his teachers said he was good at math. They said he should take advanced math classes. So he did, even though he didn't really like math. When he graduated from college, he told his father, "I want to travel. I want to see Africa." His father did not make eye contact. He said, "You're good at math. You could make a lot of money. Maybe you can be an engineer. Or do something in finance, say, be an investment banker."

HOME

MENU

DISPLAY

BACK

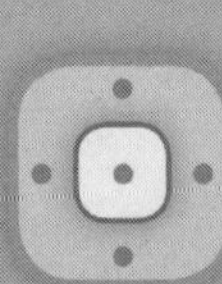

3 So Lucas became an investment banker. He did not travel. He did not see Africa. He fell in love and was thinking about having a family. "I'll travel later," he thought. And so he was an investment banker, and he tried hard to enjoy it. He got married. His family grew. The years passed by. It was a good life, but he did not travel. He did not see Africa.

4 Soon Lucas wasn't an investment banker anymore, but a retired investment banker with nothing to do. To make matters worse, he was a retired investment banker who forgot things. He forgot to turn off the oven, to bring in the mail, to take his medicine. Then he started forgetting more important things, like what his children did for a living and what his grandchildren's names were, and how many he had. He no longer acknowledged his neighbors – he had forgotten their names, too. And he forgot that he had once thought about venturing to Africa.

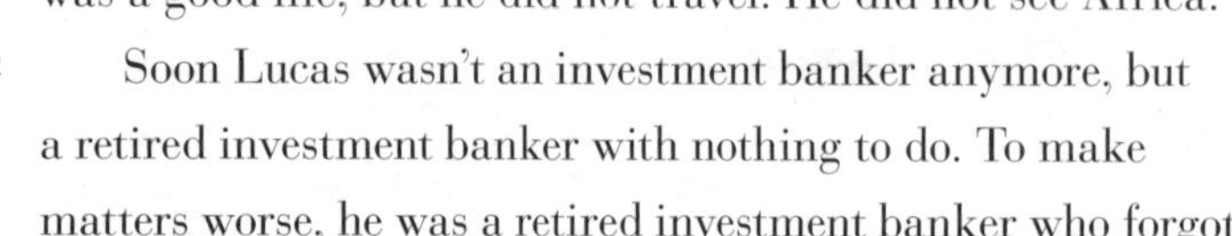

5 Then one afternoon when he had gone outside for a walk, Lucas looked up at the sky and forgot what his mother had told him. He forgot he was not a lion. He made his way toward a spot in the warm sun and lay down. He stretched out his big lion paws and felt a light breeze in his mane. He blinked his large lion eyes. A puffy white cloud was slowly making its way across the sky. He watched it until it had evaporated in the warm African air.

B Check your understanding **Write the number of the paragraph next to each description.**

1. Lucas is a middle-aged man who is struggling with his choices. ______
2. He is getting old, and it is having a negative effect on his memory. ______
3. He is young and carefree. ______
4. He must choose a career. ______
5. He is at the end of his life. ______

C Read for main ideas **Choose the correct option to complete the sentences.**

1. Lucas's mother yelled at him because she was ______ .
   a. having dinner b. annoyed with him c. scared of lions
2. Lucas's father didn't make eye contact because he wasn't ______ .
   a. happy with Lucas's plans b. sure of his advice c. interested in Lucas
3. In paragraph 3, we learn that Lucas ______ .
   a. didn't want to travel anymore b. traveled for work c. didn't like his job
4. In paragraph 4, we learn that Lucas ______ .
   a. was enjoying his retirement b. had an illness c. hated investment bankers
5. We learn in paragraph 5 that Lucas ______ .
   a. finally traveled to Africa b. was very old c. could no longer see

D Focus on vocabulary **Replace the words and phrases in bold with words from the story.**

1. Lucas **put** his hands **down hard** on the table. (para. 1)
2. Lucas's mother pulled him away from his sister by **pulling on** his shirt. (para. 1)
3. Lucas's grandfather **moved** a dish of ice cream across the table. (para. 1)
4. When Lucas told his father he wanted to travel, his father didn't **look him in the eye**. (para. 2)
5. His father suggested he should be, **for example**, an engineer or an investment banker. (para. 2)
6. When Lucas got older and started forgetting things, he no longer **said hello to** his neighbors. (para. 4)
7. Lucas forgot that he had thought about **going somewhere risky**, **for example** to Africa. (para. 4)
8. He **walked** to a place in the sun and lay down. (para. 5)

E React **Read the story again and answer the questions.**

1. Which goals did Lucas achieve? Which goals did he not achieve?

______

______

2. Why do you think Lucas became an investment banker?

______

______

3. Why do you think Lucas never traveled to Africa?

______

______

Writing A narrative article

A Read the sentences in the box. Where do they belong in the narrative article below? Write the numbers 1–5.

1. I reached for my wallet and realized it was gone.
2. I was feeling a little tired and distracted.
3. I've often thought about that woman.
4. I live in a big city, so I'm pretty careful with my belongings.
5. She called my credit card company, which contacted me.

☐ I don't really lose things. But during the holidays last year, I was looking for gifts for my family at a large department store.

☐ After hours of searching, I found a few gifts and was standing in line to pay. ☐ I looked everywhere – I even went to the lost and found department – but my wallet was nowhere to be found.

I just started shaking. There had been about $500 in my wallet – my whole budget for the holidays! I finally gave up and left the store. About 15 minutes later, my phone rang.

A woman had found my wallet on a scarf display. ☐ She had seen all the cash and felt panicked for me. All the money was there when she returned my wallet, which is amazing. She said she'd never even thought about keeping the money. And even though I was really just thankful to have my wallet and all my credit cards back, I admit that I'd been worried about losing all that money.

☐ I guess that there are still honest people in this world – people who do the right thing.

B Complete the narrative with appropriate forms of the verbs given.

It __________ (be) safe to assume that flights these days are going to be crowded. I usually __________ (prepare) myself for the worst. But the last time I traveled, I was amazed at how rude people were. I __________ (sit) quietly in my seat, and I __________ (read) a book. The man who __________ (sit) next to me __________ (hit) me with his elbow at least 20 times. Then the woman in front of me suddenly __________ (push) her seat back. She __________ (hurt) my knees and __________ (spill) my drink! The flight attendant __________ (bring) napkins, but I was totally soaked. Since then, I __________ always __________ (take) the train whenever possible!

C Editing Correct the mistakes in this narrative. There is one error in each sentence.

I have always ~~spoke~~ spoken to store clerks, but they don't always acknowledge me. One day I shop in a clothing store and needed help with a size. I have said, "Excuse me," but the salesperson ignored me. Finally, a manager was seeing me and asked if she could help. It was a good thing that someone finally helped me because I hadn't knew the sizes were for teenagers! Since then, I haven't went back to that store.

D Write a narrative article for an online magazine about a time you experienced unexpected behavior from someone. Include an introduction, background events, main events, and a conclusion. Then check your article for errors.

Listening extra Stories behind things

A Think of a special possession, and write notes about it. Answer the questions.

- How did you get it? ____________________
- When did you get it? ____________________
- Does it remind you of (make you think of) anyone or anything? ____________________
- Is there a story behind it? ____________________

B Listen to Justin talk about items on his bookshelf. Check (✓) the three items he talks about.

☐ ☐ ☐ ☐ ☐

C Listen again and complete the chart.

	Justin's possession	How did he get it?	When did he get it?
1.			
2.			
3.			

D Listen again. Answer the questions.

1. Which item does Justin keep as a memory of . . .
   a. a person? ____________
   b. a great time with friends? ____________
   c. a life lesson? ____________
2. Which item . . .
   a. does Justin use regularly? ____________
   b. is not really his? ____________
   c. did he get most recently? ____________

E Use your notes in Exercise A, and imagine you are telling a friend about your special possession. Write a short conversation.

____

____

____

____

Now complete the *Unit 3 Progress chart* on page 98.

Unit 4

Working lives

Lesson A Vocabulary Verb + noun collocations

A Match the two parts of each sentence. Write the letters a–f.

1. Employers like applicants who ____
2. Applicants should show that they are good at ____
3. Make sure you've done your homework on a company ____
4. If a candidate has training in a specialized area, ____
5. A résumé should highlight ____
6. If you have ideas about ways to save money for a company, ____

a. making progress and achieving goals on a project.
b. the résumé should clearly highlight it.
c. describe them in the interview.
d. show interest in the company and not just in the job itself.
e. before you submit an application.
f. the skills and knowledge a candidate has acquired in school or at another job.

B Complete the advice column from a career website. Use the correct form of the verbs in the box.

achieve	follow	make	show
face	have	meet	✔ submit

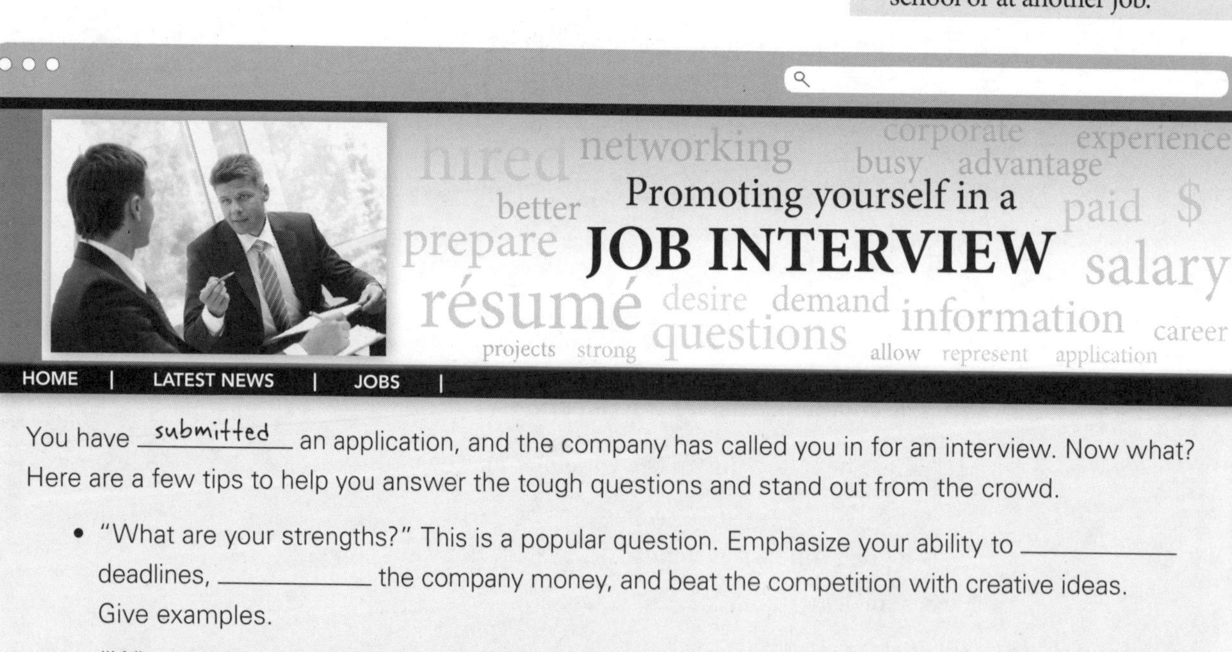

You have submitted an application, and the company has called you in for an interview. Now what? Here are a few tips to help you answer the tough questions and stand out from the crowd.

- "What are your strengths?" This is a popular question. Emphasize your ability to ____________ deadlines, ____________ the company money, and beat the competition with creative ideas. Give examples.
- "What are your weaknesses?" Always answer this in a positive way. Give an example of a weakness, explain how you deal with it, and show your willingness to ____________ advice.
- "Why should we hire you?" This is an opportunity to highlight any training you ____________. It is also important to describe how you can collaborate with others to ____________ goals.
- "Do you have any questions?" Always have at least one question ready to ask the interviewer. Make sure you have done your homework before the interview, and ask intelligent questions about the company and the job. You are probably ____________ stiff competition, and this ____________ your interest in the company.

At the end of the interview, thank the interviewer and ask for a business card. Don't forget to follow up a few days later with a thank-you email.

Lesson A Grammar Types of nouns

A Complete the conversation with a correct form of the nouns given. Add *a/an* or make the noun plural, where necessary.

Macy Hey, Jack, could you help me with something, please? I need ____________ (advice)!

Jack Sure. What's up?

Macy Well, I'm putting together ____________ (application) for a job as a personal assistant, and I need ____________ (feedback) on my résumé. I wonder if you could give me some ____________ (comment).

Jack OK, let me see. Well, you've got ____________ (information) here about your last job at the clothing store, but there's not much here about the ____________ (training) you've had as a receptionist. I think that's more important.

Macy Yeah, I guess that *is* ____________ (detail) I could add. Receptionists and personal assistants do similar ____________ (job). I mean, they do similar types of ____________ (work).

Jack Have you talked to anyone who is ____________ (personal assistant)? In the interview, you'll need to show that you have some ____________ (knowledge) of the job.

Macy Yeah, I got ____________ (help) from ____________ (counselor) at an agency. She was really nice.

Jack Great. Well, it sounds like you're all set, then.

B Complete the sentences with the correct simple present form of the verbs.

1. Today, more and more highly qualified candidates ____________ for low-level jobs. (apply)
2. A lot of work experience ____________ always necessary to land your dream job. (not be)
3. The research you do ____________ an employer that you're interested in the company. (show)
4. Be sure all the relevant information about your jobs ____________ on your résumé. (appear)
5. A lot of graduates from my school ____________ careers in education. (choose)
6. Specialized knowledge ____________ often necessary for jobs in science and engineering. (be)

About you

C Complete the questions with a correct form of the nouns and verbs given. Then answer the questions with information that is true for you.

1. What personal ____________ (information) ____________ (be) appropriate on a résumé?

   ____

2. Who have you asked for help with your résumé? What ____________ (feedback) ____________ (be) the most helpful?

   ____

3. What ____________ (be) some of your most important career ____________ (goal)?

   ____

4. What special ____________ (knowledge) ____________ (be) necessary to do your dream job?

   ____

5. What ____________ (training) ____________ (be) required for careers you're interested in? Or ____________ (be) there any special ____________ (training)?

   ____

Lesson B Grammar Generalizing and specifying

A Look at each noun or noun phrase in bold. Is the speaker making a generalization (G) or talking about a specific person or thing (S)? Write G or S.

1. "Could you please send **the feedback** on my résumé to my personal email address?" ____
2. "Sometimes **advice** that contradicts your own ideas is hard to take." ____
3. "I always take my gym clothes to **the office**." ____
4. "I would just really love a health club right in **the building**." ____
5. "When I find **a company** that offers **good health insurance**, I'll be happy." ____ ____
6. "**The advice** you gave me was invaluable." ____

B Complete the blog post with *a/an, the,* or – (no article).

BLOG | PODCASTS | PROGRAMS | LISTEN LIVE

So, most of you know I'm looking for ____ job. And most of you know that I haven't had much luck so far! Well, I've decided to write ____ description of my dream company, just in case anyone is reading! :-) My dream company has ____ office with ____ window for each employee. It offers ____ good benefits, like ____ health insurance. In the building, there are ____ great perks – like ____ gym with ____ sauna, and ____ room where employees can lie down and take ____ nap. ____ Spanish classes at lunchtime are free, and you can take ____ other classes after work. This company lets you listen to ____ music in ____ office, but you shouldn't disturb others. And it's family friendly: It offers ____ child care, and if ____ kids want to come hang out with you at lunch, that's OK, too.

So what do you think? What's your dream company like? What are ____ perks and benefits that you'd like?

posted Sunday, July 24 at 8:13 p.m.

About you

C Answer the questions with information that is true for you.

1. What is more important to you, a high salary or a lot of vacation time? Why?

____

____

2. Do you like to listen to music at work, or do you prefer peace and quiet? Why?

____

____

3. Would you rather have paid overtime or flexible work hours? Why?

____

____

Lesson C Conversation strategies

A Complete the conversation with the adverbs in the box. Use each adverb only once.

clearly	interestingly enough	seriously	unfortunately

Chris Do you think I'll ever find a job?

Mara Oh, Chris! Are you kidding?

Chris ____________, I'm getting discouraged.

Mara Don't worry. Something will come up. You're working hard, ____________. I mean, you're sending out résumés every day!

Chris Well, I'm emailing résumés to companies that haven't actually advertised job openings. You know, companies I researched and would like to work for. I just don't know if I'm making any progress.

Mara Yeah, but you never know. ____________, I just saw something about this on a career website. It said employers like candidates who've done their homework on the company.

Chris I guess so. I would just love some positive feedback.

Mara Well, ____________, it just might take some time.

B Circle the appropriate response to complete each conversation.

1. *A* Do you ever feel stuck in your job? I mean, do you wish you could do something else?
   B Well, not really. In fact, **I'm looking for something right now / I really love my career choice**.
2. *A* Does your company offer subsidized transportation to and from work?
   B Yeah, and as a matter of fact, **I need to use it more often / they offer discounted transportation**!
3. *A* How's your job search going? Have you found anything?
   B I've had several offers but not the right one yet. In fact, **I rejected an offer today / I haven't found a job**.
4. *A* Is it difficult to find work these days?
   B Actually, no. In fact, they say **there are more jobs than ever / there's really high unemployment**.

C Complete the conversation. Write the letters a–e.

Alma I'm thinking about changing careers. I don't make enough money teaching economics. ______

Felipe Yeah, but your job is so "you." ______

Alma Yeah, luckily, I do love teaching. ______

Felipe You could ask for a raise. ______

Alma I can't really do that. But I could do some tutoring, I guess. ______

a. Seriously, you can't tell me you'd leave teaching just to get a better salary.
b. In fact, I think I'll start looking into it.
c. But unfortunately, with my salary, I just can't save any money.
d. Clearly, I should get a job at a bank or something.
e. Oddly enough, sometimes all you have to do is ask.

Lesson D **Reading** Job offers

A **Prepare** **How important to you are the factors below when you are evaluating a job offer? Give each factor a number from 0 (not at all important) to 10 (extremely important).**

- ☐ the cafeteria
- ☐ company culture
- ☐ opportunities for training
- ☐ opportunities to travel on business
- ☐ opportunity to work from home
- ☐ where the company is
- ☐ your boss's personality
- ☐ your personal wants and needs

B **Read for main ideas** **Read the post from a career website. Which of the factors in Exercise A are mentioned?**

IS THIS JOB RIGHT FOR ME?

Evaluating a job offer

1 So, you've just been offered a job. The long, difficult search is over, right? Well, maybe not. As a matter of fact, you haven't faced the real challenge yet. When you get a job offer, it's hard not to get excited and just accept it. But don't let your excitement make you forget about the importance of this decision.

Of course you'll think about salary and benefits as you evaluate a job offer. But how do you decide if a particular job is right for you? Interestingly enough, salary and benefits might not be the most important factors to consider. Here are some things to think about as you make your assessment.

2 ☐ Obviously, you're going to think about yourself when you make your decision. But be careful not to make a decision based on someone else's opinion. For example, don't take a job because your parents or friends think you should. This is the time to put a high value on your own wants and needs. You will be the one who has to go to work and do the job every day.

3 ☐ What is this company really like? Do employees seem to like one another and collaborate well together? Clearly, this is hard to see if you don't already work for the company, but you can assess some things in very little time. How did you feel during your interviews at the company? Do people seem happy? Are their workspaces bright and welcoming? Did you notice anything that made you uncomfortable? If a voice in your head is warning you about the company culture, it's a good idea to listen to that voice.

4 ☐ Does the job honestly seem interesting to you? Will it challenge you? Will there be a need for some of the skills and training you have from previous jobs or internships? You'll be spending more than 2,000 hours a year at work. Certainly you want that time to be challenging and rewarding.

5 ☐ Will you have a chance to acquire skills and knowledge you don't already have? Are there opportunities for you to get new training? Most importantly, is there a good chance that you'll get promotions and work your way up in the company over time? You'll want to think about long-term as well as short-term career growth.

6 ☐ Your boss can make your job a wonderful experience or a terrible one. Will you be able to learn from this person? Will he or she offer guidance and give constructive criticism, and help find a solution whenever difficult problems pop up? If so, this may be the right fit for you. However, if you feel that you and your boss won't get along, this can have a negative effect on your performance, and unfortunately, you might have to look elsewhere.

7 ☐ Your potential new job is in a busy city (but you feel overwhelmed by large cities), and your daily commute will be long (and possibly crowded). Or the company is located too far from a city center (and there are no shops or cafés around). If either of these is true, is it OK with you?

There are many factors you need to consider when assessing a job offer. It's also a good idea to get some specialized advice and guidance from a career counselor or a professional you know. If you examine these factors, along with salary and benefits, you are on your way to making the best decision you can.

C Information flow **Where do these headings fit in the article? Write the letters a–f in the boxes in the article.**

a. Company culture
b. Location
c. Opportunities for growth
d. The position
e. Your new boss
f. Yourself

D Focus on vocabulary **Complete the nouns in bold with the correct endings. Use the article on page 30 to help you.**

1. You should consider the **imp**____ of training and opportunities to learn new things. (para. 1) ❑
2. One way to make an **assess**____ of a company's culture is to look around at people's workspaces. (para. 1) ❑
3. If you put a high **val**____ on your free time, you should ask about vacations and days off. (para. 2) ❑
4. If you have a **ne**____ for specialized advice, you should see a career counselor. (para. 4) ❑
5. You should take a lot of **gui**____ from other people before you accept any job. (para. 6) ❑
6. Getting constructive **critic**____ from a boss will have a negative effect on your performance. (para. 6) ❑
7. According to the article, the **sol**____ to the problem of finding the right job is straightforward. (para. 6) ❑

E Read for main ideas **Decide if the sentences in Exercise D are true, false, or if the information is not given in the article. Write T, F, or NG in the boxes above.**

About you

F React **Answer the questions with information that is true for you.**

1. In your opinion, what are the two most important reasons for rejecting a job offer?
____
____
2. What do you think are the two most important things to look for in a company's culture?
____
____
3. Why do you think it's important to acquire new skills at work?
____
____
4. Is company location important to you? Why or why not?
____
____
5. Who do you go to for advice when making important decisions? Why?
____
____

Writing A personal statement

A Read the excerpt from a personal statement on a job application. In what order do these topics appear? Number the topics 1–5.

introduction ___	studies ___	work experience ___
leisure time ___	summary ___	

I have been interested in international relations since I took an economics class in my junior year of high school. I started an exchange program at my school, and during my senior year, I organized an exchange with a group of students from Mexico City. **I decided** to study international relations in college because **I was interested** in a wide range of subjects, including global economics, political science, international law, and finance. Last summer, I had an internship at an international law firm. **I was responsible for** attending client meetings and writing reports. My manager **guided** me, and I received training in planning and making assessments. In my free time, I volunteer at an immigrant center. This work has been invaluable because I have met people from all over the world and helped them **solve** their various problems. I am ready to use my skills and knowledge in a challenging work environment. I feel my education and experience have prepared me for a position with an international company.

B Rewrite these sentences from Exercise A with the noun forms of the words in bold.

1. My interest in international relations began when I took an economics class in my junior year of high school.
2. ______________ to study international relations in college was based on ______________ in a wide range of subjects . . .
3. ______________ included attending client meetings and writing reports.
4. I received ______________ from my manager.
5. I have met people from all over the world and helped them find ______________ to their various problems.

C Editing Correct the sentences. There is one error in each sentence.

1. During my internship, I learned how to use all the latest softwares that designers use today.
2. Last summer, I received a training in new information systems.
3. I received constructive advices from my manager, which helped me improve my skills.
4. I am looking for a work in a technology company.
5. I gained an experience in solving clients problems.

D Write a personal statement for a job application. Then check your personal statement for errors.

My interest in architecture began in high school and was encouraged by my art teacher . . .

Listening extra A career expert

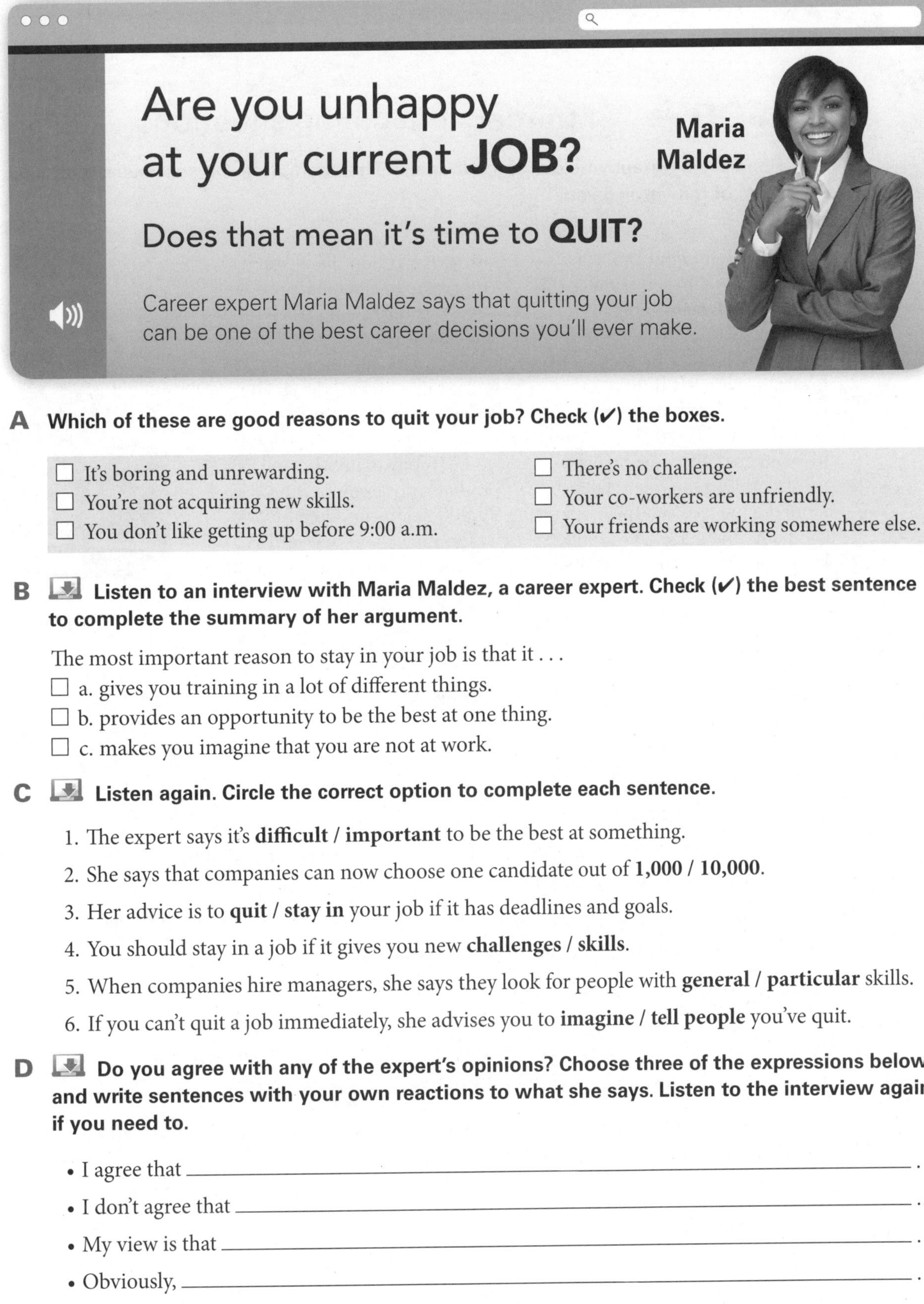

Are you unhappy at your current JOB?
Maria Maldez
Does that mean it's time to QUIT?
Career expert Maria Maldez says that quitting your job can be one of the best career decisions you'll ever make.

A Which of these are good reasons to quit your job? Check (✔) the boxes.

- ☐ It's boring and unrewarding.
- ☐ You're not acquiring new skills.
- ☐ You don't like getting up before 9:00 a.m.
- ☐ There's no challenge.
- ☐ Your co-workers are unfriendly.
- ☐ Your friends are working somewhere else.

B Listen to an interview with Maria Maldez, a career expert. Check (✔) the best sentence to complete the summary of her argument.

The most important reason to stay in your job is that it . . .

- ☐ a. gives you training in a lot of different things.
- ☐ b. provides an opportunity to be the best at one thing.
- ☐ c. makes you imagine that you are not at work.

C Listen again. Circle the correct option to complete each sentence.

1. The expert says it's **difficult / important** to be the best at something.
2. She says that companies can now choose one candidate out of **1,000 / 10,000**.
3. Her advice is to **quit / stay in** your job if it has deadlines and goals.
4. You should stay in a job if it gives you new **challenges / skills**.
5. When companies hire managers, she says they look for people with **general / particular** skills.
6. If you can't quit a job immediately, she advises you to **imagine / tell people** you've quit.

D Do you agree with any of the expert's opinions? Choose three of the expressions below and write sentences with your own reactions to what she says. Listen to the interview again if you need to.

- I agree that ________________________________.
- I don't agree that ________________________________.
- My view is that ________________________________.
- Obviously, ________________________________.
- The expert's right to say that ________________________________.
- I don't think that ________________________________.

Now complete the *Unit 4 Progress chart* on page 99.

Unit 5

Challenges

Lesson A Grammar Imagining situations

A Read the biography below of a billionaire. Then complete the sentences with a correct form of the verbs given.

When John Paul DeJoria was in high school, his classmates voted him "Least Likely to Succeed." Even a teacher told him, "You'll never be successful." Later his wife left him and their two-year-old child. At one time, DeJoria was so poor that he and his young son became homeless.

Luckily, a few years later, he landed a job as a salesperson at a company that made hair products. He worked hard and made a lot of money for the company, but he lost that job and several other jobs afterward because of his unusual ideas. He then used the skills and knowledge that he had acquired to collaborate with a hairstylist friend, Paul Mitchell, and create his own hair products.

After borrowing $700 to start the business, DeJoria lived in his car for several weeks. He had no money for advertising, so he promoted the products himself by going from salon to salon. Today, Paul Mitchell products are in more than 90,000 salons in 82 countries. DeJoria is now very wealthy: He's worth more than $4 billion.

DeJoria has given millions of dollars to charities around the world. He says donating money to charity is effective, but "so is showing up and doing something."

John Paul DeJoria

1. If DeJoria had listened (listen) to his teacher, he ______________ (might not become) so successful.
2. DeJoria ______________ (might not be) so successful now if he ______________ (not lose) some of his jobs.
3. If he ______________ (not collaborate) with a hairstylist, his products ______________ (not attract) the attention of so many salons.
4. If DeJoria ______________ (not become) homeless, he ______________ (might not learn) to care about other people's problems.
5. He ______________ (might not be) so well-known now if he ______________ (not be) so generous with his fortune.

About you

B Complete the questions with a correct form of the verbs given. Then answer the questions using conditional statements and your own ideas.

1. __________ you __________ (be) confident now if a teacher __________ (say) to you, "You'll never be successful"?

   ____

2. If you __________ (be) in DeJoria's situation many years ago, how __________ you __________ (feel) if you __________ (lose) a number of jobs?

   ____

Lesson B Vocabulary Problems and solutions

Complete the conversations with the words in the boxes.

create	creation	investment	invests	poor	✔ poverty	wealth	wealthy

1. *A* Look at that homeless woman with her children. It's so depressing. Poverty is such a huge problem in this city. So many ____________ families are struggling.
   B I know. The distribution of ____________ is a real issue. I can't believe how incredibly ____________ some people are. Seriously, what do they *do* with all that money?
   A I know what you mean. Clearly, the government ____________ in job ____________, but it seems that the jobs they ____________ are either low paying or highly specialized.
   B Yeah, I wish there were more ____________ in education and job training. Then more people would have a chance.

eradicate	eradication	invest	investment	starvation	starving

2. *A* Do you know anything about investing? We've been thinking we want to ____________ in companies that give back to the community in some way.
   B You mean that do charitable work? Or companies that make vaccines or something to ____________ childhood diseases? I know some companies that are working towards the ____________ of malaria.
   A Yeah. That or companies that help people who are ____________, for example.
   B Right. ____________ is a huge problem. Well, hmm, you probably should check it out online. But it's a great idea – making an ____________ in socially responsible companies can make a big difference.

distributing	distribution	hunger	hungry	unemployed	unemployment

3. *A* What did you do this weekend?
   B Oh, the usual. On Sunday I worked at the food bank ____________ food.
   A Really? I didn't know you were doing volunteer work.
   B Yeah. You know, I can't just do nothing when people are ____________. Our food bank is responsible for the ____________ of more than 5,000 meals a week, which is a lot for a small town.
   A Wow! I didn't realize that ____________ was such a problem here.
   B It's pretty serious. And with very high ____________ rates, the situation isn't getting any better. Fortunately, though, not all the people who come to us are homeless. Many have homes, but are ____________, you know, they're struggling to find a job.

eradication	pollution	protect	protection

4. *A* I'm so tired of reading about large corporations polluting the environment.
   B I know. I just can't understand why ____________ is still a problem in this day and age! I mean, don't people realize we all have to ____________ the environment? Why don't governments pass stricter environmental ____________ laws? That should be easy.
   A Well, not really. It's expensive to do things the "green" way.
   B But if greener methods lead to the total ____________ of pollution, we all win.

Lesson B Grammar Wishes, hopes, and regrets

A Circle the correct form of the verbs to complete the sentences.

1. I'd forgotten that my friend's husband had lost his job. I really wish I **hadn't brought up / didn't bring up** the unemployment issue when we were having lunch last week.
2. The distribution of wealth is so imbalanced in this country. I hope the government **would do / will do** something about it in the near future.
3. I wish more people **would stop / stop** buying bottled water. It would go a long way toward protecting the environment.
4. I hope this year's political debates **include / would include** the pollution issue. We have so many polluted rivers in our area!
5. I wish the government **could / will** eradicate poverty in our country.
6. My responsibilities at work include buying gifts for clients. I wish I **will have signed up / had signed up** for the green committee instead.

B Read the conversations. Complete the responses with a correct form of the verbs given. Sometimes more than one answer is possible.

1. *A* You know, the government doesn't do enough to protect the environment.
   B You're absolutely right. I wish environmental protection ________ (be) a top priority.
2. *A* There are so many hungry children in our country. It's very sad.
   B I know. I wish the government ________ (spend) more to eradicate hunger. It's just not a priority for them right now.
3. *A* Did you hear about the most recent unemployment numbers? The rate is the lowest in history.
   B That's great news! I just wish it ________ (get) that low last year when a lot of my friends were looking for jobs.
4. *A* Do you think they'll ever find a solution to the city's traffic problems?
   B Who knows? But I hope they ________ (invest) in some new buses. The old ones are always breaking down.

About you

C Complete the sentences with your own ideas.

1. Water pollution is a huge problem all over the world. (I hope . . .)
   I hope governments will work together to clean up our polluted rivers and oceans.
   ____
2. Starvation is such a huge problem in the poorest countries. (I hope . . .)
   ____
3. There's a shortage of housing. They just haven't built enough homes. (I wish . . .)
   ____
4. There are not enough good jobs for people. (I wish . . .)
   ____

Lesson C Conversation strategies

A Complete the conversation with the expressions in the box. Use each expression at least once. Sometimes more than one answer is possible.

imagine	suppose	what if

Anne A friend of mine is having a surprise party for her husband. Instead of gifts, she's asking people to bring books to donate to the local library. Cool, huh?

Raj ___________ people don't have any used books that are in good condition?

Anne Well, ___________ you were invited to the party. What would you do?

Raj You know me: I have tons of books at home, so it wouldn't be a problem.

Anne I guess most people would rather buy books than other things – like clothes and stuff. ___________ someone threw a party for you and asked people to do something for a charity? Would you be upset if you didn't get gifts?

Raj Me? No way. I really don't need a thing.

B Check (✓) the appropriate response in each conversation.

1. *A* The problem for me with holidays is all the gifts you have to buy. It's just so expensive.
   B ❑ I suppose. It doesn't cost very much, though.
   ❑ I suppose it is. Though I just set a budget and stick to it.
2. *A* Would you ever return a gift and get the money instead?
   B ❑ I don't think so. I suppose it wouldn't seem right.
   ❑ Yeah, I suppose I would. It's nice to keep the gift.
3. *A* I like to buy gifts in local stores. It's nice to support small neighborhood businesses.
   B ❑ That's true. I suppose it's better to go to a large shopping mall or something.
   ❑ I suppose it is. You can get unusual things, too. The big stores all have the same stuff.

C Complete the conversation with *suppose, imagine, I suppose, I imagine,* and *what if . . . ?* Sometimes more than one answer is possible.

A I don't know what to do with all these toys. They're in great condition, but the kids don't play with them anymore.

B Well, ___________ we donated them to that homeless shelter downtown?

A Actually, that's a great idea. I mean, ___________ you were a homeless child: even one toy would make you happy, ___________ .

B Yeah, I just wish more people would think about the homeless situation in our city. People have too much, and they give too little. ___________ everyone gave just one used toy or a book or even an old coat?

A And if people gave more, ___________ the shelter would be so much more comfortable.

B Which is why we should go take these toys down to the shelter right now.

A Yeah. Let's do it.

Lesson D Reading Medical charities

A Prepare **What problems do you think international medical charities help with? Check (✔) the boxes below.**

- ☐ building homes for the homeless
- ☐ cleaning up rivers and lakes
- ☐ clearing up after natural disasters
- ☐ finding jobs for the unemployed
- ☐ preventing disease
- ☐ treating illnesses

B Read for main ideas **Read the article. Which of the issues in Exercise A are mentioned in the article?**

The work of an international medical charity

1 Every year thousands of international volunteers – doctors, surgeons, nurses, dentists, clean water experts, and other professionals – are sent by medical charities to help local medical workers. Here we talk to a few volunteers about their experiences.

2 *LINDA JONES, a nurse, was one of hundreds of volunteers who flew to a devastated area after an enormous earthquake.*

3 *Q* **Do people usually come together during a disaster?**

A The devastation after the earthquake was just huge. Large parts of the region were completely destroyed, but the community really did come together. I suppose it might be surprising, but in my experience most people help each other during natural disasters. As we were clearing up we found a woman, for example, who was looking after a neighbor's five-month-old baby and her two-year-old sister. Their mother was too sick to take care of them, and their father was devastated. But he also had to work. . . . If the neighbor hadn't helped, the father wouldn't have been able to work, and he might have lost his job. There are lots of stories like this. I don't know what we would have done if we hadn't had this kind of help with the sick and injured from the community.

4 *Another volunteer, TIM MENDES, a general surgeon, helped to remove injured patients from a war zone.*

5 *Q* **How do you safely remove the injured from war zones?**

A It always depends. Recently I worked with a team to get people out of a dangerous area by boat. There was a large number of patients, so our idea was that it would be quicker to get them out by a floating ambulance. Many had life-threatening injuries. We had several doctors and nurses, and even one dentist who had some emergency medical training. Everyone was helping.

6 It was a difficult journey. Everyone was seasick. We had to take care of people, but we couldn't even stand up! The boat trip was 10 long hours, but it was amazing when we landed safely and there were 18 ambulances waiting to take the patients to the hospital.

7 Despite the bad weather and the rough conditions on the boat, it was a successful operation. If we hadn't used a boat, a lot of people wouldn't have been saved.

8 *DR. MARGARET WINTERS is a project coordinator at a large international medical charity.*

9 *Q* **What happens when there isn't enough money or resources to treat illnesses?**

A It's a real problem and I wish there were an easy solution because millions of people continue to suffer and die from common diseases that could be prevented. In a lot of the countries that we work in, we see people with lumps and growths that become enormous. This simply wouldn't happen in wealthier countries. Often they're not malignant, you know they're benign tumors, but without treatment they cause a lot of suffering for the people concerned. We're always hoping that governments will invest more in our work.

C Read for main ideas **Read the article again. Who talks about . . .**

1. health care in poor countries? ______________
2. patients with serious injuries? ______________
3. a family? ______________
4. a floating ambulance? ______________
5. the need for more resources? ______________

D Focus on vocabulary **Choose the word that best completes each sentence.**

benign	devastation	injured	treatment
dentists	enormous	sick	tumor
devastated	huge	surgeons	

1. International volunteers include many medical professionals such as doctors, ______________, nurses, and ______________ .
2. After a ______________ earthquake, doctors flew to the regions that were most affected by the ______________ .
3. People often come together after a natural disaster even though they all feel ______________ by what has happened.
4. It's important that doctors are able to help the ______________ and ______________ as soon as possible.
5. It can be an ______________ problem to remove sick people from war zones.
6. A small lump can quickly turn into a large growth or ______________ . Sometimes it's ______________ and not harmful or malignant, but it's still a problem.
7. In richer countries, patients receive ______________ for common health problems earlier.

E Read for detail **Are the sentences true or false? Write T or F. Correct the false sentences.**

1. Linda Jones was not surprised that people came together after the earthquake. _____
2. The neighbor helped the father find a job. _____
3. The dentist only helped people who had problems with their teeth. _____
4. They used 18 floating ambulances to remove people from the war zone. _____
5. There is not an easy solution to finding money and resources to treat illnesses. _____
6. In richer countries people have the same health problems as in poorer ones. _____

F React **Answer the questions about the article. Give your own views.**

1. What do you think about these volunteers and the work they do?

____

____

2. Whose job was the most difficult do you think? Why?

____

____

3. If you were able to volunteer, what kinds of work would you prefer to do?

____

____

Writing An inquiry

A Read the email inquiry. Add *it* where necessary in the underlined parts of the sentences.

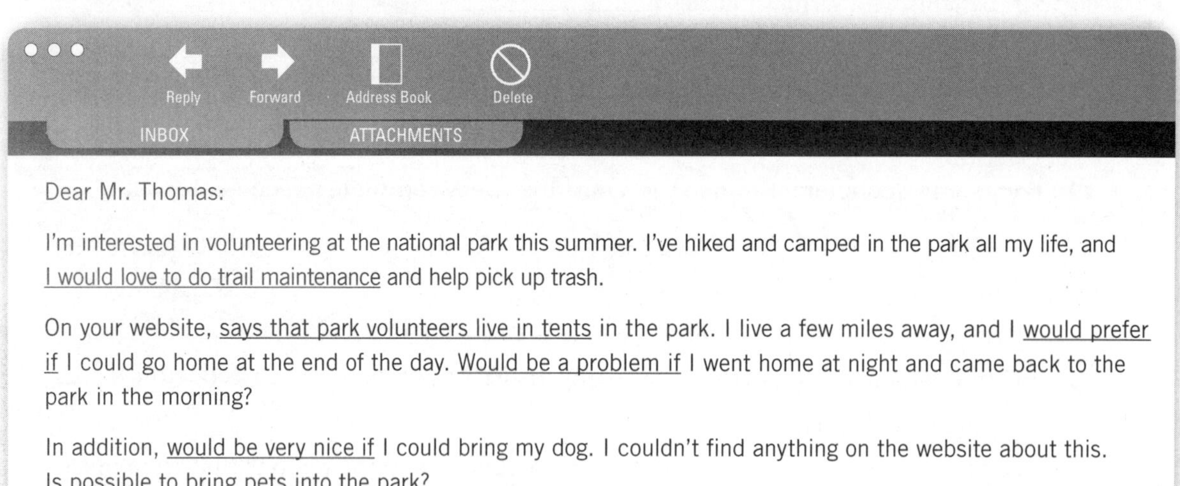

Dear Mr. Thomas:

I'm interested in volunteering at the national park this summer. I've hiked and camped in the park all my life, and I would love to do trail maintenance and help pick up trash.

On your website, says that park volunteers live in tents in the park. I live a few miles away, and I would prefer if I could go home at the end of the day. Would be a problem if I went home at night and came back to the park in the morning?

In addition, would be very nice if I could bring my dog. I couldn't find anything on the website about this. Is possible to bring pets into the park?

I would appreciate if you could send me more details about the volunteer program and the application form for volunteers. Thank you for your attention. I look forward to hearing from you.

Sincerely, Carlos Almieva

B Unscramble the sentences.

1. if / could / a current volunteer / It / useful / would be / I / speak to

   ______________________________.

2. if / begin working / I / love / immediately / could / would / it / I

   ______________________________.

3. if / a problem / it / when I arrive / Would / paid / I / be

   ______________________________?

4. more information / it / you / I / send me / appreciate / would / if / could

   ______________________________.

C Editing Correct these sentences. There is one error in each one.

1. Will be interesting to read about your training program.
2. Would be a problem for me if I had to wait another week to start?
3. Is difficult for me to commute on the bus.
4. Would be useful if I could arrive a day early?
5. Was interesting to read your website.

D Write an email inquiry to a volunteer program. Use an idea in the box or your own idea. Then check your email for errors.

read books to children at a literacy center	volunteer at a city park
teach a craft at a homeless shelter	volunteer at a home for the elderly

Listening extra Making a difference

A Rewrite the sentences by replacing the words in bold with the words in the box. Then answer the questions with your own ideas.

charitable organization	connected	donors	requests	support

1. Would you like to **give money to** a charity more often?
   Q: ______________________________
   A: ______________________________
2. What's the name of your favorite **charity**?
   Q: ______________________________
   A: ______________________________
3. How do charities stay **in touch** with **the people who give money**?
   Q: ______________________________
   A: ______________________________
4. How often do you get **letters that ask** for donations?
   Q: ______________________________
   A: ______________________________

B Listen to an extract from a TV show. Check (✔) the sentences that give the speaker's views.

- ☐ She wishes people would stop supporting some charities.
- ☐ She thinks the only way to help a charity is to give money.
- ☐ She thinks local charities often find it hard to raise money.
- ☐ She hopes she'll be able to do more projects in the future.

C Listen again. Complete the sentences with no more than three words.

1. Sunny has always felt strongly about world issues like poverty and the ______________ .
2. People tend to stop giving to charity because they don't know what happens to ______________ .
3. Small charities who are looking for money for projects can ______________ on Sunny's website.
4. People who give small amounts of money still like to feel that they are ______________ .
5. Some donors like to give to college students who are ______________ .
6. A new kindergarten just received $1000 for ______________ .

About you

D Answer the questions with your own ideas and opinions.

1. What do you think about Sunny's idea?
   ____
2. Is it better to support international charities or ones in your own area? Why?
   ____
3. What are some other ways charities can stay connected with the people who support them?
   ____

Now complete the *Unit 5 Progress chart* on page 99.

Unit 6

Into the future

Lesson A Grammar Describing future events

A Use the words given to write sentences about future events.

1. We / will / be / live / in a totally cashless society by 2050.
We'll be living in a totally cashless society by 2050.
2. People / won't / be / use / credit or debit cards.
3. Everybody / be going to / be / do / their banking online.
4. People / won't / be / write / checks anymore.
5. We / be going to / be / carry / around fewer gadgets generally.
6. Everyone / will / be / do / all their grocery shopping on the Internet.

B Circle the correct option to complete the conversation.

A Hey, did I tell you? My boss said I'm going to get a new tablet for work!

B Lucky you! What **are you using / are you going to use** it for?

A Well, **I'll take / I take** it with me if **I'll visit / I visit** clients. But I guess when **I need / I'll need** to do a lot of typing, **I still use / I'll still use** my laptop.

B So, do you think tablets **replace / will replace** laptops in the future?

A Well, I don't think laptops **are going to disappear / disappear**, but they probably **won't be / aren't** as popular in the future.

B I suppose we **might use / use** them less if tablets **will become / become** more common.

A Yeah. I suppose that's inevitable.

About you

C Answer the questions with your own ideas.

1. What device(s) do you think you'll be using for work and for fun in five years from now?
2. Do you think one device will ever replace all the devices people use now? Why or why not?
3. Design your dream device. What will it be able to do?

Lesson B Vocabulary Expressions used in presentations

A Read the beginning of a presentation. Write the letter of each expression a–h in the appropriate place.

Good morning. I'm Liu Peng, director of the Global Conference on the Future of Technology. Thank you for coming. Today's speaker is an expert in the field of transportation engineering. Her designs have won awards in cities all over the world. So ☐ to her now. Everyone, please welcome Helena Lopes.

Thank you, Liu Peng. Good morning, everyone. Um, ☐ in the back? OK, great. Oh, and did you all pick up a handout by the door on your way in? If you don't have one, raise your hand because ☐ now. Everybody has one? Great.

Today, as part of our series on the future of technology, ☐ the future of transportation, and in particular, trains. ☐ my talk by taking a general look at transportation issues in both urban and rural areas, and talk about possible solutions. After that, ☐ and look at new developments in transportation technology. Please save your questions for later, as ☐. There's a lot of information to present, and I want to get through it all. So ☐. (. . .)

GLOBAL CONFERENCE ON THE FUTURE OF TECHNOLOGY

Rio de Janeiro, Brazil

MAY 21–25

Helena Lopes

a. I want to look at	e. let's get started
b. I'd like to begin	f. we'll move on
c. I'll allow time at the end	g. they should be going around
d. can everybody hear me	h. I'll turn it over

B Complete the end of the presentation with the words in the box.

comments	questions	stop
handout	saying	time

(. . .) So, as you'll see on page 10 of the __________, there are many new technologies that promise to help solve tomorrow's transportation problems. And as I have shown today, trains will be contributing in large part to those solutions.

Well, since it's almost 3:00, I'd better __________ there, because that's all I have __________ for today. I'll just conclude by __________ that you're going to be seeing a lot of exciting new changes in train transportation in the future. So, um, does anyone have any __________ or __________?

Lesson B Grammar Modal verbs

A Complete what the presenter says. Match each sentence with the most logical second sentence. Write the letters a–d.

1. Does everyone have a handout? ______
2. So, let's move on and watch a short clip. ______
3. OK, we're running out of time. ______
4. We have to stop now. ______

a. I'd better stop here and answer your questions.
b. Thank you for coming.
c. Everyone should have one by now.
d. Could somebody turn the lights off, please?

B Circle the best option to complete the extracts from a presentation.

1. **Can / Would** everyone hear me? If not, I **might want to / could** turn up the sound.
2. The sound's not on? The microphone **must / had better** be turned off. **Would / Must** someone check it for me? Thanks.
3. Now, everyone **might want to / ought to** have a handout by now. If you didn't get one, you **might want to / would** share with the person next to you.
4. So, **would / can** I ask a question? How many of you **had better / can** pay all your bills online?
5. Well, it's 11:30, so we**'d better / would** stop here. The next group **might / won't** be waiting for the room. Thank you for coming.

C Use the modal verbs in the boxes to rewrite the underlined parts of the presentations.

✔ might want to	need to	ought to	won't	would

1. OK, let's move on. Now I want to look at different ways we'll be conserving energy in the future. (**a**) I advise you to move to the front so you can see the screen. (**b**) Somebody turn the lights off, please. (**c**) Um, it's necessary for me to find the clip on the computer. (**d**) I believe it's on my desktop. (**e**) Oh, it's failing to open. I'll go onto the next one.

   a. You might want to move to the front so you can see the screen.
   b. ______________________________
   c. ______________________________
   d. ______________________________
   e. ______________________________

can	had better	might want to	should	will

2. (**a**) Is everyone able to see the chart on page 2 of the handout? (**b**) I believe everyone has a handout by now. (**c**) I can't explain these numbers in detail today, but I advise you to look up the information on our website. (**d**) If no one has any questions, I'm offering to give you a few more resources. (**e**) Then it's necessary for us to stop.

   a. ______________________________
   b. ______________________________
   c. ______________________________
   d. ______________________________
   e. ______________________________

Lesson C Conversation strategies

A **Check (✓) the places where you can add one of the softening expressions in the box.**

I would say / I'd say	I would think / I'd think	I would imagine / I'd imagine

Isabella Wow, ☐ did you hear? The *Times-Journal* is going paperless.

Sou-Chun Yeah, no more actual newspaper. You know, ☐ all newspapers are going to be doing this in the near future, fortunately.

Isabella I suppose. Though ☐ a lot of people still like to hold a real newspaper in their hands. For example, ☐ my mom says she gets headaches when she reads on a screen.

Sou-Chun Really? I prefer the online versions. But ☐ reading on a screen will get easier pretty soon. You know, ☐ screen technology will probably get more advanced.

Isabella ☐ I hope you're right. But ☐ in the end, people will support anything that's better for the environment.

Sou-Chun Exactly. And it's cleaner – ☐ newspapers always get my hands dirty!

B **Circle the best expressions to complete the conversations.**

1. *A* What if all doctors could treat patients over the Internet? I mean, do you think that we'll all eventually be treated online – like, without seeing a real doctor?
   B **I don't think so. / I hope so.** There are a lot of illnesses that need the personal attention of a doctor.

2. *A* I get all my news from the Internet. I haven't read a newspaper in ages – and I don't miss it.
   B So, do you think that newspapers will all be online soon?
   A **I guess so. / I hope not.** Newspapers are struggling. Don't you think they'll eventually die out?
   B **I hope so. / I hope not.** I'll always want the *option* of reading a real newspaper.

3. *A* Do you think people will play more virtual-reality sports in the future?
   B **I guess so. / I hope not.** But they'll still play sports with their friends. It's a social thing.
   A But it can still be a social thing if you play with friends online.
   B Yes, but it's not the same as getting together, say in a park, and playing baseball or something.
   A **I guess not. / I think so.** Being outside is part of the fun.

4. *A* I heard that a restaurant near here is going to have tablets on every table. So we'll be ordering food without the waiter. Do you think that'll catch on?
   B Oh, **I hope so. / I guess not.** That'd be fun. It'd probably be quicker, too!

C **Circle the best expressions. Then write softening expressions to complete the conversation. There may be more than one possible expression you can use.**

A There are so many people with e-readers now! Do you think books will disappear completely?
B **I hope not. / I guess not.** I'm not ready to read everything on a screen.
A Yeah, but ________________ e-readers are more practical. Think of all the books you can carry around!
B **I hope so. / I guess so.** I wonder if the screens will become interactive, like if you could talk to them or something. That would make it quicker to find things.
A ________________ they will. I mean, computers and tablets are getting more interactive, so ________________ the same will happen with e-readers, too.

Lesson D Reading Important challenges for our future

A **Read for main ideas** **Read the report from a conference on future technological challenges. Then write the correct headings in the report. There are three extra headings.**

clean energy	communication	public health
clean water	poverty	public housing

Future technological challenges

1 As the world's population grows, one of the most difficult challenges we face is to improve our quality of life. Clean energy, disease prevention, and access to clean water are some of the most important aspects of this challenge, according to a group of leading experts at a recent world conference on technological advancement.

2 **1.** ______________________

Earth's growing population is consuming its resources too quickly, experts say. Scientists have emphasized the need to develop new sources of energy, while at the same time protecting the environment. Economists predict that oil prices will likely continue to rise, and consumers, especially large corporations, retailers, hospitals, and schools will be looking for cheaper sources of energy, such as solar power. The sun gives off more energy in one hour than the entire world population consumes in one year. However, the challenge for inventors is to convert solar power into useful forms, and to store it inexpensively.

3 **2.** ______________________

As more and more people live longer, there will be a greater demand for medical treatments that are effective, cheap, and available to everyone. Scientists are finding new ways to understand how the body works, and this new understanding could well lead to more personalized treatment. Personalized medicine will undoubtedly have enormous benefits to public health because it will help doctors and therapists to identify a patient's health problems earlier and treat them successfully. This should also reduce medical costs to patients.

4 **3.** ______________________

Climatologists and ecologists predict that a change in weather patterns will inevitably affect the planet in significant ways. Some areas will likely experience severe droughts, whereas others will see heavy flooding. Drought and floods can both lead to a shortage of clean drinking water and food and create an increase in refugees and migrants as people move to new areas in search of food or clean water. More investment in new technologies will undoubtedly be needed to make water safer in difficult times.

5 The above challenges cannot be met without economic support. All too often, cheaper technologies that pollute the environment are still preferred over cleaner, more expensive ones. On the last day of the conference, one expert concluded by saying, "If industries and governments don't invest in new technologies, we're going to destroy our planet and the people who live here. Earth's resources won't last forever and we might well become victims of our own lack of planning. Spending millions now might well save billions later."

B Check your understanding **Answer the questions. Check (✔) a, b, or c.**

1. What was the main theme of the recent conference?
   - ☐ a. finding ways to stop the population growing
   - ☐ b. improving the quality of life for people
   - ☐ c. sharing technologies
2. According to the report, what is one of the biggest challenges in using solar power?
   - ☐ a. There is not enough for our needs.
   - ☐ b. It is not environmentally friendly.
   - ☐ c. It is expensive to store.
3. What is one of the benefits of personalized medicine?
   - ☐ a. Treatment will be shorter.
   - ☐ b. Patients will have more access to treatment.
   - ☐ c. Treatment will be less expensive.
4. Which of these is not mentioned in the report as a result of the effects of climate change?
   - ☐ a. Areas will experience water shortages.
   - ☐ b. Rain will become more polluted.
   - ☐ c. People will have to leave their homes.
5. What is needed to meet the three challenges in the future, according to the report?
   - ☐ a. more inventors
   - ☐ b. less spending by governments
   - ☐ c. more investment in technology

C Focus on vocabulary **Complete the definitions with words from the report.**

1. ________ study the distribution of resources and the production of goods and services. (para. 2)
2. ________ sell things, and ________ buy them. (para. 2)
3. ________ create or design new things. (para. 2)
4. Doctors and ________ treat people with health problems. (para. 3)
5. ________ study weather and climate. (para. 4)
6. ________ study the natural relationships between the air, land, water, animals, plants, etc. (para. 4)
7. ________ go to other places or countries because they are escaping from a dangerous situation. (para. 4)
8. ________ are people who go to live in another place or country. (para. 4)
9. ________ are people who suffer the effects of something. (para. 5)

About you

D **Answer the question.**

One important message from the report is "You have to spend money to save money." Do you think this is true? Why or why not?

____
____
____
____
____
____
____
____
____

Writing A one-paragraph article

A Number the sections in the correct order to form a one-paragraph article. Then label the topic sentence (T), the supporting sentences (S), and the concluding sentence (C).

[ ] ______ Doctors and patients will benefit from these new technologies, which will undoubtedly make health care more effective and more convenient.
[ ] ______ New technology in medical care will undoubtedly give doctors more reliable information about a patient's health, and may well make visits to the doctor's office less frequent and possibly less unpleasant.
[ ] ______ Another exciting invention is a "pill-cam", a tiny wireless camera that patients swallow and which sends images of any health problems to their doctor's computer screen.
[ ] ______ One example of this technology is the "tele-health monitor". This piece of equipment, which patients will have in their homes, will constantly check a patient's health and send instant information to a doctor. When there is a problem, the doctor will call the patient immediately.

B Complete the article by adding the adverbs in parentheses.

undoubtedly

In the future, medical treatment, even in the poorest countries worldwide, will ^ change to a system that starts before a patient gets sick. (undoubtedly) In the near future, doctors will be able to collect millions of pieces of information about a child shortly after birth. (likely) People will find out at an early stage if they will get sick in later life. (inevitably / eventually) However, with the kind of information that technology can give them, people may be able to take action to prevent illnesses until much later in their lives. (well) These advances will improve the quality of life and health of many people throughout their lives. (ultimately)

C Editing Complete the sentences with the adverbs in the box. Choose an adverb that adds the idea in parentheses. Sometimes more than one answer is possible.

actually	currently	eventually	maybe	recently	ultimately

1. Technology will ______________ bring better treatments to everyone.
   (I'm sure this will happen in time.)
2. Doctors are ______________ testing a new treatment for heart disease.
   (They are doing this now.)
3. The government has ______________ invested in a hospital-building program.
   (They did this last year.)
4. Many people will ______________ not want to know about their future health problems.
   (This is a fact.)
5. If technology develops, there will ______________ be no human doctors.
   (This will happen in time.)
6. ______________ in the future, we will be able to eradicate all disease.
   (I'm not 100 percent sure.)

D Write a one-paragraph article about a prediction for the future. Use the ideas above or your own ideas. Include a topic sentence, supporting sentences, and a concluding sentence. Then check your one paragraph article for errors.

Listening extra Challenges in the 21st century

A Write the captions in the boxes under the slides.

Rising sea levels | The Arctic Ocean | The construction industry | Greenland

1. ☐ ______
2. ☐ ______
3. ☐ ______
4. ☐ ______

B Listen to the lecture. Check (✓) the three topics in Exercise A that are included in the lecture.

C Listen again and complete the student's notes.

The 2007 United Nations study:

- estimated ocean levels would rise between ______ and ______ inches (= 18 to ______ centimeters)
- did not include the impact of ______ ______ – in particular in Greenland (then sea levels could rise by at least ______ ______, or 5 meters)

The new study from Norway estimates that:

- sea levels could rise by ______ feet (1.6 meters) by ______
- the Arctic Ocean will have ______ ______ during the summer

Talk will cover four impacts of rising sea levels:

1. Environmental impact – the effects on ______ and ______
2. Effect on climate – especially ______ and storms
3. Impact on ______ supplies
4. The ______ impacts, especially on ______ and fishing

About you

D Answer the questions about the information in the lecture.

1. Which information did you already know?
______
2. Did any information surprise you?
______
3. What other information have you read recently on this topic?
______

Now complete the *Unit 6 Progress chart* on page 99.

Unit 7

Getting along

Lesson A Vocabulary House rules

A Circle the best option to complete the house rules.

Rules for dormitory living

1. If a problem comes **up** / **over** / **off**, please call the building manager.
2. If you make a mess, clean it **up** / **to** / **over**.
3. If you see trash on the floor, pick it **on** / **over** / **up** and throw it away.
4. When you leave your room, be sure to turn **over** / **off** / **back** the lights.
5. Talk quietly in the hallways so you don't wake people **over** / **forward** / **up**.
6. If you have friends **with** / **over** / **out**, they must leave the building by 11:00 p.m.

B Complete the two parts of the conversation with the expressions in the boxes.

come up with	go over	✔ look forward to	put off	wake up

Ji Ning I never look forward to our house meetings. But I guess tonight's meeting is important. There are so many things we need to __________ .

Clara I agree. Things haven't been going well lately. We should have had the meeting weeks ago. I don't know why we __________ it __________ so many times.

Ji Ning Well, part of the problem is Jasmina. When she's here, all she does is sleep. I try to be quiet because I don't want to __________ her __________ , but it's not really possible to have a life when someone next door is sleeping all the time.

Clara Well, we have to __________ a plan. If we don't, we'll be fighting all the time.

clean up	give back	give up	have over	put up with	run out of

Jasmina Sorry I'm late, guys. I've been working overtime – again. I wish I could __________ my job __________ , but you know how much I need the money.

Ji Ning OK, so let's start our meeting. So, we were just saying that we don't want to have to be quiet all afternoon just because you're sleeping. We __________ it because we know you're tired, but . . .

Jasmina OK, OK. I get it. But can I say something? Clara, you need to do the dishes more often. I hate it when we __________ clean plates and glasses. It happens all the time. Everyone loves to __________ friends __________ , but you have to __________ afterwards.

Clara You're absolutely right. Oh, before I forget, Jasmina, could you __________ my DVD __________ ? You know, the one you borrowed last week?

Jasmina Of course. I'll get it right now.

Lesson A Grammar Using phrasal verbs

A Unscramble the words in parentheses to complete the house rules.

1. When you have to get up early, try not to ______________ .
   (the entire household / up / wake)
2. When you ______________ , be considerate and don't make too much noise. (friends / over / have)
3. ______________ on time for house meetings. (up / show)
4. If we ______________ , replace it quickly. (out / run / something / of)
5. If you are the last one to watch TV, ______________ before you go to bed. (it / turn / off)
6. If you borrow things from your roommates, don't forget to ______________ . (back / them / give)
7. Let's ______________ the bills together so everyone knows how much to pay. (go / over)
8. If you disagree, try to ______________ without arguing. (with / up / come / solutions)

B Complete the anecdote with the words in parentheses. Write them in the correct order and place. Sometimes more than one answer is possible.

My roommate's just so annoying – she wakes me ^up every morning. (up) She's always running cash and forgets to pay the bills. (of / out) She never shows when we have a meeting with the building manager. (up) Then, whenever she cooks, she always puts cleaning her mess. (off / up) Sometimes she won't do a thing for days! Will this work? (out) I'd love to come up a solution to this problem, but I don't think that I can put with her bad habits any longer! (with / up)

About you

C Complete *B*'s responses with a correct form of the phrasal verb that *A* uses. Add the pronouns *them* or *it*. Then answer the questions with your own ideas.

1. *A* Do you usually put up with your friends' annoying habits?
   B I generally put up with them – as long as they put up with mine!
   ____
2. *A* Do you often put off chores?
   B Yeah, I hate doing chores. I ______________________ as long as I can.
   ____
3. *A* How do you get over an argument with friends or family?
   B Oh, I usually figure out a way to ______________ . You know, sometimes humor helps.
   ____
4. *A* How likely are you to give up a bad habit when someone is constantly commenting on it?
   B Well, it depends! If it's a really bad habit, I'll try to ______________ .
   ____

Lesson B Grammar Describing experiences

A Circle the correct form of the verbs to complete the childhood memory.

As an only child, my mother had always wanted siblings **to play / playing** with. When she and my father got married, they agreed it was important **to have / having** more than one child. So they had six kids! Things weren't always easy, though. For example, there was never anywhere quiet **for / to** sit in our house. But I always had fun **to hang out / hanging out** with my older sisters. My brother was the only boy, so he was often bored **to play / playing** with girls all the time. And you know, I think he was a bit lonely **to be / being** surrounded by so many girls. But mostly, we had no problem **to grow up / growing up** in such a big family, and we're all still very close.

B Complete the conversations with a correct form of the verbs given. Sometimes more than one answer is possible.

1. *A* You were an only child, right? Weren't you bored playing (play) by yourself all the time?
   B Sometimes. But there were a lot of families in my building, so there was always a neighbor's apartment __________ (go) to.
2. *A* Was it tough __________ (grow up) with so many kids in the house? Did you argue a lot?
   B No, not really. We had no problem __________ (get along). There weren't enough toys __________ (play) with, so we learned that it was important __________ (share).
3. *A* My dad worked a lot when I was a kid. When he came home from the office, he was always really tired and it was hard for him __________ (find) any time for me.
   B So do you think you had problems __________ (connect) with him?
   A Well, yeah. My mother had lots of time __________ (spend) with me, but I think it was difficult for her __________ (be) almost like a single mom.
4. *A* Do you think it's worth __________ (wait) until you're like 38 to have children?
   B Oh, it depends. My parents had fun __________ (travel) before they had me. But I had kids when I was pretty young and had no trouble __________ (raise) them. It's impossible __________ (say) what's better.

About you

C Answer the questions with information that is true for you.

1. Do you think that it's important for children to have siblings? Why or why not?

   ____

   ____
2. Who did you play with when you were growing up? What did you play?

   ____

   ____
3. When you were growing up which family members did you have problems getting along with? Who did you have no trouble getting along with? Why?

   ____

   ____

Lesson C Conversation strategies

A Choose the appropriate responses to complete the conversation.

Emma Did I tell you I moved out of my parents' house last week?

Jayne Really? That's wonderful! I mean, it must be __________ .

a. great having your own place   b. difficult living on your own

Emma Yeah, I couldn't wait. I'm not saying __________ . It's just that I was ready, you know?

a. I hated living with my parents   b. I want to live with my parents

Jayne Yeah. And now you can have people over! What I mean is, __________ .

a. you can come over to see me   b. you'll have fun hanging out with friends

Emma Yeah, but to tell you the truth, I'm just a little nervous about cooking for myself every day. I mean __________ .

a. I never cooked much at home   b. I cook all the time

Jayne Oh, it's not even worth worrying about. What I'm saying is, you'll __________ .

a. have problems with it   b. be fine. It's no big deal

B Complete the conversations with the sentences in the box. There is one extra sentence.

To tell you the truth, my friends gave the best advice.
I have to say, it's much easier financially.
Well, I'm an only child, and to be honest, it was lonely.
Honestly, parents are more likely to tell you what you need to hear.

1. *A* I think it's good for kids to grow up in big families. You know what I mean?
   B I don't know. I grew up in a big family, and I have to say, it's not always easy competing for your parents' attention.
   A ______________________________

2. *A* I read online that kids take more advice from their friends than from their parents.
   B I suppose that's true. I always went to my friends for advice, which wasn't always a good idea.
   ____

3. *A* This is so embarrassing! I graduated two years ago, and I'm still living at home.
   B Yeah, but lots of people our age still live at home. ______________________________

C Complete the conversation with the sentences below. Write the letters a–e.

Samia My older brother still lives at home, and my parents pay for everything! It's just not fair. ___

Marek Yeah, that seems pretty unfair. ___

Samia I've never asked my parents for anything. ___

Marek Yeah. The thing is it could cause problems between you and your brother. ___

Samia You're right. You know what? I'm going to talk to him about it tonight. ___

a. I don't mean that they wouldn't help me if I asked, but I try to be independent.
b. I have to say, it's tough if your parents are giving your brother more support than you.
c. What I mean is *I* pay for everything myself, and I think he should too, to be honest.
d. I mean, if I don't say anything, the problem will only get worse.
e. And quite frankly, you don't want money problems stopping you from getting along.

Lesson D **Reading** The perfect roommate?

A **Prepare What is your idea of a perfect roommate? Write four ideas. Then scan the article to see if any of your ideas are mentioned.**

How to get rid of the PERFECT ROOMMATE

1 So you've moved out of your parents' house for the first time, and if you're like most young people on a tight budget, chances are that you probably have a roommate. But what's your roommate like? Does he or she consult you before having friends over? Or clean up all the mess in the apartment? That's obnoxious! If a problem comes up, does your roommate come up with an idea for solving it? Well, don't worry. There's a way to deal with that.

2 Are you seeing other eccentric behavior, too – with the chores, for example? Does your roommate do them every day and never put them off? This sets a bad example for everyone! To make things worse, your roommate is probably never short of money (that's just not normal if you're a student, right?) and always pays the bills on time. When you and your friends from college go out, your roommate would never tag along with you – not without an invitation. Right? Don't you think that's a little weird?

3 If any of this sounds like your roommate, then you have one who's just too perfect – and that's no good! It's tough living with someone you can't argue with and who doesn't complain. That's just no fun! You need to get rid of this roommate, and you shouldn't put it off. If you let this person stay too long, these bad habits could start to rub off on you.

4 But all is not lost. If you follow these suggestions, you'll have no trouble getting your roommate off your back.

5
- Set your alarm for 5:00 a.m., and turn it off every five minutes until you're ready to get up for class – two hours later.
- Tell your roommate you'll take out the trash, and then never get around to it.
- Make it impossible for your roommate to have time alone with friends. When he or she has friends over, talk loudly on your cell phone and refuse to leave the room until you drive them away.
- Come up with great ideas for meals, but then don't make them. Forget to go to the supermarket, and then suggest ordering a pizza – again. When the pizza delivery guy comes, ask your roommate – who always has money – to pay. You have a student loan to pay off and other things to worry about, right?
- Make sure your roommate always has chores to do and never has any free time. When he or she's not looking, undo the chores he or she just did. For example, collect bottles and cans in your closet. Fill the empty recycling bin with them right after your roommate has taken out the recycling.
- Run out of cash right before it's time to pay the rent. Borrow money from your roommate, and then pay it back – $5 at a time.
- Let your roommate down regularly. For example, invite him or her to a friend's party, but don't give him or her the address. Then disappear all day and come home late, talking about the fabulous time you had.

6 These techniques should help you get rid of your perfect roommate forever. After all, you don't want someone to help with the chores. Quite frankly, you don't want anyone to do the chores. You want to put them off as long as you can. I mean, why clean up a mess when you could be studying. Right?

B Read for style **Check (✔) the true statements about the article.**

☐ 1. It is aimed at families who don't get along.
☐ 2. It has advice on getting along with roommates.
☐ 3. It says the opposite of what is true.
☐ 4. It is written for parents.
☐ 5. It is not a serious article.
☐ 6. It is useful advice.

C Understanding reference **Find the sentences in the article. What do the underlined words refer to?**

1. That's obnoxious! (para. 1) ____________
2. . . . does your roommate come up with an idea for solving it? (para. 1) ____________
3. Does your roommate do them every day and never put them off? (para. 2) ____________
4. This sets a bad example for everyone! (para. 2) ____________
5. Don't you think that's a little weird? (para. 2) ____________
6. That's just no fun! (para. 3) ____________
7. . . . and refuse to leave the room until you drive them away. (para. 5) ____________
8. Fill the empty recycling bin with them . . . (para. 5) ____________

D Read for detail **Find these sentences in the article. What do they mean? Check (✔) a or b.**

1. This sets a bad example for everyone! (para. 2)
   ☐ a. Your roommate should always put off doing chores, because everyone does.
   ☐ b. If other people start behaving the same way as your roommate, you'll have to as well.

2. It's tough living with someone you can't argue with and who doesn't complain. (para. 3)
   ☐ a. Your roommate is just too nice. You want a *normal* roommate.
   ☐ b. Your roommate is so lazy, it's driving you crazy!

3. If you let this person stay too long, these bad habits could start to rub off on you. (para. 3)
   ☐ a. Over time, this person's good behavior will force you to be a better roommate.
   ☐ b. Over time, this person's bad habits will make all your roommates behave badly.

E Focus on vocabulary **Find the expressions below in the article. Then complete the sentences with the expressions.**

be short of	get around to	let down
drive away	get off your back	tag along with

1. It's important for you to share the chores and the bills. You don't want to ____________ your roommate ____________ and end up living alone.
2. Let your roommate ____________ you occasionally when you go out.
3. If your roommate doesn't ____________ doing the dishes, it's not worth worrying about.
4. Be a good roommate: try not to ____________ your roommate ____________. A promise is a promise!
5. It's impossible to ____________ an annoying roommate ____________ without hurting his or her feelings. If you have problems, talk them through. He or she will thank you for it!
6. Budget carefully. You don't want to ____________ money, especially at the end of the month when there are bills to pay.

Writing An introduction to an essay

Essay question

A recent research paper states: "Children don't try to copy adults as much as we think – they're trying to be like other children." This implies that other children have a greater influence on a child than his or her parents. Do you agree or disagree with this statement?

A Read the introductory paragraph to an essay. Underline the thesis statement.

Most people agree that a child's personality is shaped by his or her environment. On the one hand, an important part of a child's environment is his or her parents and their parenting style. Children learn some important lessons from their parents. On the other hand, a child's need to get along in a group influences his or her behavior even more. In my opinion, what is most important in the end is the social behavior that children learn from their friends.

B Rewrite the underlined part of each sentence with a *What* clause.

1. Children need to fit in with one another.
   What children need is to fit in with one another.
2. It is clear that friends have the strongest influence on a child's personality.
   ____
3. It is essential to guide your child's choice of social groups.
   ____
4. This means that a child's parents are not as important as his or her friends.
   ____
5. It is likely that parents play a more insignificant role in their child's emotional development.
   ____
6. Children perceive that their friends are the people who are most like them.
   ____

C Editing Correct the sentences. There is one error in each sentence.

1. Is important to help your child choose his or her social groups wisely.
2. What means is that friends have a strong influence on a child.
3. Is clear that children aren't interested in becoming copies of their parents.
4. What implies is children teach one another to be social.
5. Is interesting that children almost always learn behavior from their friends.

D Write an introduction to the essay question. Include a thesis statement. Then check your introduction for errors.

Listening extra *Ask Alison!*

A **Look at the list of complaints about people. Which of the complaints are problems for you? Give each complaint a number from 0 (not a problem) to 10 (a big problem) in the first column.**

Common complaints about people	Me	The callers
a. He/She never returns your calls.	☐	☐
b. He/She is always late.	☐	☐
c. He/She never helps clean up after dinner.	☐	☐
d. He/She tags along without an invitation.	☐	☐
e. He/She takes up all your free time.	☐	☐
f. He/She is always borrowing money.	☐	☐

B **Listen to the call-in radio show. Number the complaints in Exercise A in the order you hear the callers mention them. There are two extra complaints.**

C **Listen again. Are the sentences true or false? Write T or F. Correct the false sentences.**

1. Mark orders in pizza or pasta for his brother. ______
2. Alison advises Mark to be direct with his brother. ______
3. Laura's problem is with her roommate. ______
4. Laura has tried to solve the problem. ______
5. Berto wants to spend more time with his girlfriend. ______
6. Alison advises Berto to plan regular date nights. ______

About you

D **Listen again. Do you agree or disagree with the advice? Write why or why not. Then write your own responses to the callers' complaints.**

1. Advice for Mark: **agree / disagree?** ______________________

   My advice: ______________________

2. Advice for Laura: **agree / disagree?** ______________________

   My advice: ______________________

3. Advice for Berto: **agree / disagree?** ______________________

   My advice: ______________________

Now complete the *Unit 7 Progress chart* on page 100.

Unit 8

Food science

Lesson A Grammar Information focus

A Complete the sentences with a correct passive form of the verbs given.

1. With global warming, it is thought (think) that harvests in some parts of the world ________ (will affect) by drought. As a result, crops that can survive in drier weather conditions ________ (must develop). Recently, crops that need less water ________ (have grown). In addition, these crops ________ (can grow) in poor soil with few nutrients.
2. In the future, it ________ (hope) that more food ________ (will sell) in the same areas where it ________ (produce). This would mean that crops ________ (will not transport) over long distances from farmer to consumer. It also means that less food ________ (would import).

B Rewrite each sentence in the paragraph in the passive without *they*.

Organic food is food that **they** grow without pesticides. **They** have practiced organic farming methods for thousands of years. It became less popular in the twentieth century as **they** invented more productive methods. **They** didn't consider organic farming effective, and **they** used more pesticides and other chemicals to increase crop yields and grow more food. More recently, however, **they** have reconsidered the value of organic farming, and **they** expect the market for organic food to grow in the future.

Organic food is food that is grown without pesticides.

____

____

C Rewrite the predictions in the passive. Start with the words given. Add *by* if necessary.

1. In countries that have food shortages, farmers are going to use improved farming methods.
   Improved farming methods ________.
2. Engineers are going to build better greenhouses so we can have longer growing seasons. Supermarkets will sell less imported fruit in the future.
   Better greenhouses ________. Less imported fruit ________.
3. Supermarkets are going to encourage consumers to buy more food that is produced locally. They're no longer going to fly food halfway around the world.
   Consumers ________. Food ________.

Lesson B **Vocabulary** For your health

A Circle the correct option to label the picture.

1. **digestive system / heart**
2. **liver / skin**
3. **heart / muscles**
4. **bones / muscles**
5. **brain / liver**
6. **muscles / teeth**
7. **heart / liver**
8. **digestive system / muscles**

B Complete the sentences with the words in the box.

brain
digestive system
heart
liver
muscles
skin

1. The ________________ removes toxins and is part of your digestive system.
2. The ________________ controls thought, memory, and feelings.
3. ________________ produce movement in your body.
4. The ________________ pumps blood around the body.
5. ________________ covers your body and protects it from disease.
6. The ________________ processes food so that it can be used by the body for energy.

C Complete the excerpts from a presentation with the words in the box.

blood pressure	digestive system	immune system	skin
bones	eyesight	metabolism	teeth

Today I'd like to talk about "functional" foods. These are foods that are considered to have extra health benefits such as strengthening your ____________ so that you can fight disease, or lowering your ____________, which is important for good heart health. Typically, "functional" foods have added nutrients. For example, calcium-fortified orange juice. As most people know, you need calcium to help prevent your ____________ from breaking, and for healthy ____________ and gums. . . .

. . . We'll move on and look at another product. Some yogurt manufacturers claim that the probiotics in their products help the stomach and ____________ to process food better. Other studies have shown some low-fat yogurts can help increase your ____________ and possibly lead to weight loss. . . .

. . . So, in the future, "functional" foods are going to become big business. We might even see cake mixes that help improve your ____________ and help you see better at night. Or drinks that contain additives that can keep your ____________ clear and healthy, and prevent it from aging so quickly.

Lesson B Grammar Describing causes and results

A Circle the correct form of the verbs to complete the sentences.

1. Using a lot of salt may cause your blood pressure **from rising / to rise**.
2. Eating too much sugar may make your immune system **work / to work** more slowly.
3. Paying attention to food labels enables you **make / to make** better choices.
4. Some people say you should let your body **tell / to tell** you what foods it needs.
5. Eating avocados may protect you **getting / from getting** heart disease.
6. Drinking a lot of water may allow you **to control / from controlling** your weight.
7. Chili peppers can keep you **to gain / from gaining** weight.

B Complete the conversation with a correct form of the verbs given. Add *from* where necessary. Sometimes more than one answer is possible.

A You know, my friend only eats raw food. It's supposed to prevent you ____________ (age), and she says it keeps you ____________ (have) problems with your digestive system.

B Isn't that because a raw-food diet enables you ____________ (digest) food more quickly? So it helps you ____________ (absorb) more nutrients?

A Yes, but I believe some foods are better cooked, like tomatoes. Cooking them lets the fiber ____________ (break down), and it allows you ____________ (get) more of the nutrients.

B Huh. Don't tomatoes protect you ____________ (get) certain types of cancer, too?

A I don't know. I heard that they can help you ____________ (control) your blood pressure.

B So they can make your blood pressure ____________ (go down)?

A Well, I don't think they cause your blood pressure ____________ (rise).

B I should eat more tomatoes. It looks like they could help me ____________ (improve) my health!

C Complete the article with the words in parentheses. Put the words in the correct order and form. Add *from* where necessary. If you can leave *from* out, write ( ). Sometimes more than one answer is possible.

Here are our top tips for staying fit and feeling great

- Drinking lots of water can ____________ (lose / help / you) weight. It increases your metabolism and can ____________ (you / eat / stop) too much.
- Are you sleeping enough? Research has shown that sleeping at least seven or eight hours a night might ____________ (protect / skin / age / your).
- Experts say breakfast is the most important meal of the day. One healthy breakfast food, cereal, might ____________ (you / get / protect) heart disease. Add some blueberries to your cereal. They will ____________ (concentrate / you / help).
- Exercise. Regular exercise is good for your heart, and it can ____________ (get / you / keep) heart disease. Exercise, such as running or swimming, can ____________ (keep / help / bones / your) stronger. Exercise also ____________ (help / have / prevent / people) health problems later on in life.

Lesson C Conversation strategies

A Complete the conversations with the best rhetorical questions in the box. Write the letters a–e. There is one extra question.

a. I mean, can that even be good for you?	d. I mean, what was I thinking?
b. I mean, where did you get that idea?	e. I mean, can't we just grow everything locally?
c. Why are their vegetables so expensive?	

1. *A* You never know where food comes from these days. Take apples, for instance. The apples I bought today are from the other side of the world! That can't be environmentally friendly. ___
   B I know. I just bought some stuff at the farmers' market. It's so much fresher than at the supermarket, but I spent a fortune. ___
2. *A* My best friend only eats raw vegetables. ___ Surely you need to eat protein and other stuff, too.
   B Oh, yeah. I tried a ten-day fast once, where you just drink juice. It was crazy! ___

B Circle the best expressions to complete what Lee says.

"So, yeah, I'm trying to improve my diet and avoid all those bad things that I love eating! So **for instance, / take** instead of drinking soda, I've started making smoothies. If you drink one every day, you're getting lots of good nutrients. I'm also avoiding eating processed foods, **look at / such as** frozen dinners, which probably have a lot of additives in them. It's not easy, though. I'm also trying to find out more about the food I eat, **like / look at** does it contain artificial colors, or where does it come from? I mean, **take / such as** fruit and vegetables, **for example / take**. What kinds of pesticides have been used on them? And **such as / look at** food packages – they make a lot of claims, but how do we know what's true? Does low-fat really mean low-calorie, **for example / such as**?"

Lee

C Complete the conversation with the rhetorical questions below. Write the letters a–e in the boxes in the conversation. There is one extra question. Then write expressions (*like, such as,* etc.) to show where the speakers are giving examples. Sometimes more than one answer is possible.

a. I mean, who wants soft bananas?	d. I mean, why would anyone go to a supermarket anymore?
b. Really, why wouldn't they?	
c. Who wants to spend all that money?	e. Who wants all those additives in their food?

Will So, Eunha, you were saying you get your groceries delivered now?

Eunha Yeah. Well, some stuff, ___like___ bread and milk. I just go online, place my order, and it's delivered the next day. It's great. I used to hate carrying all those heavy bags. And it saves time. ☐

Will So how about fresh stuff? I mean, ______ fruit, ______. It's nice to choose it. ☐

Eunha Well, if you don't like something, they'll take it back. ______, I had some tomatoes that were too soft one time and they just replaced them. No problem. ☐

Will But what about reading labels on stuff? You can't do that online. I mean, ______ yogurt. Everyone thinks it's healthy. But some kinds are full of sugar and food coloring. ☐ You really have to read the labels on everything!

Eunha Well, I just order my usual things, ______ milk and cheese and stuff. So, . . .

Lesson D Reading Know your pests

A **Prepare** **In what ways are ants pests? Scan the online article, and underline evidence of ants as pests.**

Ants: are they all bad?

1 There are more than 12,000 species of ant around the world. They are generally thought of as pests – just go to any supermarket, and you will find a variety of products designed to help you get rid of them. It is certainly annoying when ants get into the kitchen or show up uninvited to a picnic, and obviously, it is painful to be stung! However, are all ants pests, or can some ants be beneficial?

2 A pest is an insect or a small animal that is a threat to the environment, the economy, or human health. □ Of all the pests in the world, fire ants are one of the most annoying – and most dangerous. These tiny red ants, originally from South America, were introduced by accident in the southern U.S. in the 1930s, where a moist and warm climate has enabled the number of ants to increase dramatically in states like Alabama and Florida. Today, fire-ant colonies cover more than 1 million square kilometers in this region and cause more than $6 billion in economic losses every year, including medical expenses and damage to crops.

3 Fire ants are aggressive, and their stings can be dangerous. □ Furthermore, the economic damage caused by the ants, which eat small plants before they have grown to full size, is devastating. This has been the painful discovery that people from the Philippines, China, and Australia have made in the last 25 years as fire ants have spread in these countries at an alarming rate, due to trade with the U.S. But why are ants a problem in these countries and not in their native South America?

4 Fire-ant colonies have been prevented from growing too quickly in South America as a result of parasites, viruses, and competition with other ant species. A lack of these natural enemies is believed to be one factor that has allowed fire ants to spread quickly in other parts of the world and is believed to contribute to their survival. □ Moreover, this growth is not slowing down: scientists believe that fire ants might well spread across half the planet.

5 So what does this mean? Is it all bad? It is well known that earthworms are a farmer's best friend. They improve the quality of farmland by turning over the soil. This helps to get air into the soil, which enables more water to be absorbed and crop production to increase. However, what many people don't realize is that many species of ant are even more beneficial to soil than earthworms. □

6 Some ants also act as natural pesticides, killing harmful crop-eating insects and protecting plants. In fact, the earliest known use of biological pest management – by Chinese orange growers – was described in a book written by Chinese botanist Hsi Han in AD 340. Bamboo "bridges" were provided by the farmers, which allowed the ants to move from tree to tree in order to reach and kill the "bad" insects.

7 Ants are also important distributors of seeds and play an important role in pollination. □ In desert areas, for example, some plants depend on ants alone to harvest and "plant" their seeds. Ants have become even more important since it was discovered that crops are being threatened by a mysterious decline in the bee population in recent years. As more bees die and their colonies collapse, ants could prevent the disappearance of bees from becoming a devastating crisis.

8 We may continue to think of ants as pests, but they perform a number of helpful jobs. It might be difficult, but try to remember this the next time you get stung by a fire ant, or an army of ants invades your kitchen.

B Read for main ideas **Where do these sentences fit in the article? Write the letters a–f in the boxes in the article. There is one extra sentence.**

a. For example, only 85 years after their introduction, there were five times more fire ants per kilometer in the U.S. than in their native South America.
b. In some cases, they can be just as effective as bees and flies in pollinating crops.
c. Queen ants can fly up to one-quarter of a mile on their own.
d. Take fire ants, for example.
e. Medical attention is sometimes required after people are stung, and small animals can even die from multiple fire-ant stings.
f. It has been discovered, for example, that the holes most ants make in the earth allow more rain to be absorbed.

C Check your understanding **Read the article again. Then answer the questions.**

1. How many species of ant have been discovered in the world?
____
2. How much does fire-ant damage cost the U.S. economy each year?
____
3. Why have fire-ant colonies spread to other countries outside of the Americas?
____
4. How do ants benefit the soil?
____
5. How do ants act as pesticides?
____
6. Why are ants considered even more important now?
____

D Focus on vocabulary **Complete the definitions with the noun forms of the verbs in the box. Find the words in the article.**

disappear	discover	lose	pollinate	produce	survive	threaten

1. Something that is a ______________ is likely to cause damage or be a danger. (para. 2)
2. If you experience ______________, you fail to keep something that is of value. (para. 2)
3. A ______________ is something that had not been known before. (para. 3)
4. The ______________ of something is its ability to stay alive. (para. 4)
5. The process of growing plants for food is known as crop ______________. (para. 5)
6. ______________ requires the deposit of pollen for fertilization. (para. 7)
7. The ______________ of something happens when it stops existing. (para. 7)

About you

E React **Were there any facts in the article that surprised or troubled you? Explain.**

____
____
____
____

Writing A report for a science class

A Look at the graphs and charts, and complete the sentences.

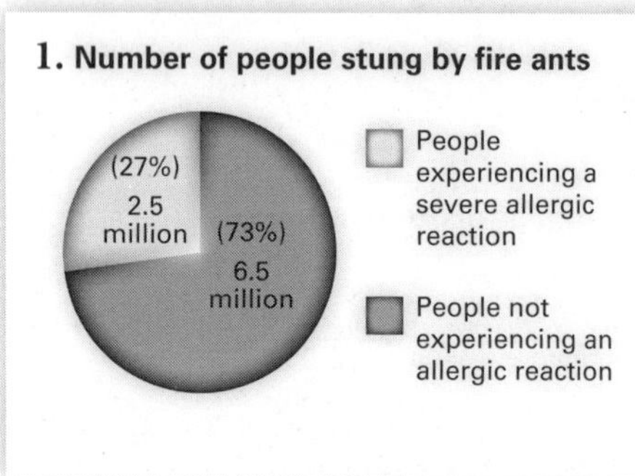

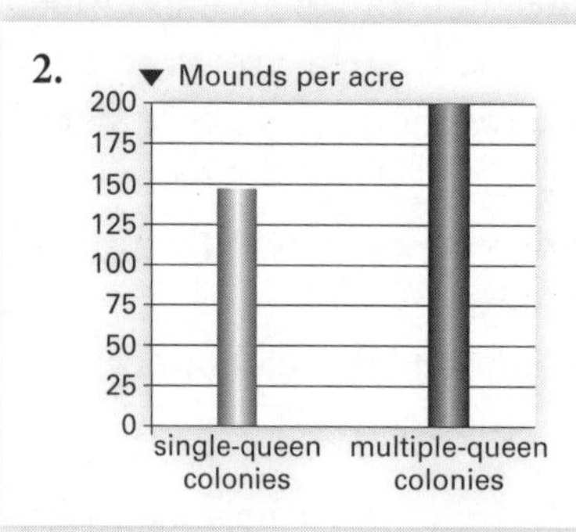

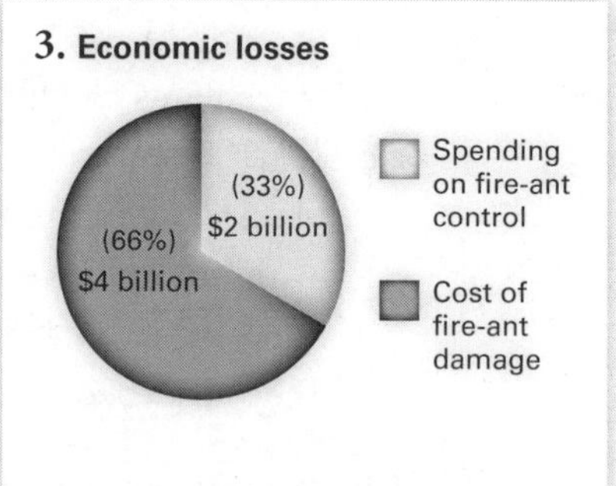

1. Approximately 2.5 million people per year experience a severe allergic reaction to fire-ant stings, which accounts for ____________ percent of all victims.
2. In areas with fire-ant colonies with just one queen, there are nearly ____________ mounds per acre. This rises to ____________ per acre in areas that have colonies with more than one queen.
3. Fire-ant control accounts for ____________ percent of the economic losses that fire ants are responsible for.

B Circle the correct preposition. Then complete the report with the expressions in the box.

+/– about / approximately / roughly	– under / less than
+ over / more than	>| nearly / almost / up to

The dramatic rise **on / in** the number of fire-ant colonies in the U.S. is a cause for concern. In areas with large fire-ant colonies, ____________ (>|) 60 percent of the population is stung every year, which means that ____________ (+/–) 9 million people are stung by fire ants each year. Of those 9 million, ____________ (+/–) 27 percent experience a severe allergic reaction and some even die.

Currently, Americans spend ____________ (+) $2 billion on fire-ant control and fire-ant damage accounts for ____________ (>|) $4 billion each year. What is worrisome is that there has been a rise **in / by** colonies that have more than one queen. Areas with single-queen colonies can have ____________ (>|) 150 mounds per acre. However, in areas with multiple-queen colonies, the number of mounds has been known to increase **in / by** ____________ (+/–) 33 percent. While the use of chemical pesticides has caused a decline **of / in** fire-ant activity **of / by** ____________ (>|) 90 percent, it has been found that the ants come back in less than one month if the pesticides are not reapplied. Some success has been reported by farmers controlling fire ants with other insects.

C Editing Correct the sentences. There is one error in each sentence.

1. The number of countries that are affected by the spread of fire ants has grown up.
2. The rise of the number of multiple-queen colonies is a cause for concern.
3. Where multiple-queen colonies are found, the number of mounds rises up significantly.
4. Chemical pesticides can cause the number of fire-ant mounds to fall down dramatically.
5. Farmers who have used other insects to control fire ants have experienced a decline of ant colonies.

D Write a report for a science class with the title *The rise in fire-ant colonies – a cause for concern?* Use the model in Exercise B to help you. Then check your report for errors.

Listening extra Smart foods

A Make a list of five foods that you think are good for you.

______ ______ ______ ______ ______

B Listen to a radio interview with an expert on food nutrition. Check (✓) the effects of foods that are mentioned in the interview. There are two extra effects.

about foods that. . .

☐ a. can improve your mood
☐ b. can prevent you from getting cancer
☐ c. can help lower your blood pressure
☐ d. can protect you against heart disease
☐ e. can prevent your skin from aging
☐ f. may protect your brain cells from deteriorating
☐ g. helps you to build strong muscles
☐ h. may make headaches go away
☐ i. may reduce the risk of depression

C Listen again. Match each smart food with its health benefits in Exercise B. Write the letters a–i. Some benefits go with more than one food.

1. blueberries ______
2. avocados ______
3. coffee ______
4. fish ______

D Listen again. Circle the best option to complete the sentences.

1. The guest on the show ______.
   a. has published books on healthy foods b. is a specialist doctor
   c. specializes in mood therapy
2. The host suggests eating avocados ______.
   a. in salads b. on sandwiches c. every day
3. Coffee has particular health benefits for ______.
   a. old people b. young people c. middle-aged people
4. Fish should be eaten ______.
   a. every day b. once or twice a week c. once a month
5. The best fish to eat is ______ salmon.
   a. farmed b. wild c. canned

About you

E Answer the questions with your own ideas and opinions.

1. Which information in the interview was new or surprising to you?

______

______

2. Does the interview make you want to eat more of any of the foods mentioned? Which ones?

______

______

Now complete the *Unit 8 Progress chart* on page 98.

Unit 9

Success and happiness

Lesson A Vocabulary Expressions with *get*

A Circle the best option to complete the *get* expressions in the article.

Caterina Fake Stewart Butterfield

Successful entrepreneurs Caterina Fake and Stewart Butterfield got **anywhere / to the top** by making their careers on the Internet. As co-founders of one of the first photo-sharing sites, Flickr, they helped change the way people use the Internet. So how did they both get **to be / under way** two of the world's most successful Internet entrepreneurs?

Caterina describes herself as "always curious," and her ability to learn new things is perhaps the quality that has helped her get **ahead / on with**. Stewart didn't study business or computer science, but he didn't let that get **anywhere / in his way**. With two degrees in philosophy, he simply got **on with / ahead** the job and learned about business along the way.

Not all products get **off to a good start / to be**, but Caterina believes that good products will ultimately sell themselves – especially on the Internet. Users of Flickr, for example, contributed to its development once it got **on with / under way**. Then, after it got **off the ground / in the way**, there was no stopping it.

So, what lessons can new entrepreneurs learn from their story? Perhaps that you won't get **anywhere / you down** by worrying about what you don't know and not to let initial problems get **off to a good start / you down**. If you know you have a great product, stay with it.

B Complete the conversation with a correct form of the *get* expressions in the box.

get ahead	get in (your) way	get off to a good start	get (me) down	get to the top
get anywhere	get off the ground	get on with	get to be	get under way

A Did you hear that I failed my final exam? It's really ______________ me ______________ . I don't know what to do. I just can't seem to ______________________ my life right now.

B I know, but you won't _____________ if you don't take control and do something positive.

A Yeah. The thing is, though, that I was sick when my classes started. So I didn't __________ . I mean, it wasn't a good way to begin the semester. Then when all the courses __________ , I felt completely lost.

B Well, a lot of successful people never graduated from college. Take Mark Zuckerberg. He dropped out of college, but he ______________ one of the richest people in the world. He managed to _________ in life and be successful. In fact, he _________ of his profession.

A I guess so. But I'm not going to ______________ a company like Facebook ______________ , am I? I mean, I couldn't start up a company like that.

B I guess not. I'm just saying don't let one failure ________________ your _____________ . Don't let it stop you from being successful.

Lesson A **Grammar** Talking about *all* and *none*

A Circle the correct determiners to complete the conversations.

1. *A* Would you say that **neither / both / all** your family members are successful in some way? I mean, like, your parents and brothers and sisters and everyone.
   B Well, I'd say that **neither / both / all** my parents are successful, because they raised a happy family. **No / None / All** family is successful if it's not happy. At least, not in my opinion.
   A I guess so. Do **none / all of / every** your brothers and sisters say the same?
   B Yeah. We all have happy memories. When we were little, **every / none of / all** kid in the neighborhood used to come to our house and **neither / each / all** kid was made to feel welcome. **None of / Neither / Neither of** my parents ever complained about how many kids were there.

2. *A* What makes a person successful, do you think?
   B Good question. If you think about **each / every / all of** the really successful actors and athletes – they work really hard to get to the top of their careers. You know, **none of / neither / no** these people just let things happen. They put in really long hours, and **all / neither / every** their hard work pays off in the end.

3. *A* How did you decide on your major? I mean, did you ask your family for advice?
   B Well, no, not really. **None of / No / Neither** my relatives went to college. So I talked to my teachers and advisors about different careers, but honestly, **no / every / none of** the information they gave me was really that useful. I think you have to choose for yourself. I mean, **none / no / each** advice is really that useful. So yeah, I looked at law and accounting and took some classes, but I decided that **all / neither / both** profession was for me.

B Rewrite the sentences by replacing the underlined words with the determiners in parentheses. Make any necessary changes to the sentences.

1. <u>Every</u> business student dreams of setting up a successful company. (All)
   All business students dream of setting up a successful company.
2. <u>All</u> the students in my class last year wanted to start a business. (Each)
   ____
3. My <u>two</u> best friends got new companies under way last year. (Both)
   ____
4. <u>Their</u> companies didn't get off to a good start. (Neither)
   ____
5. My <u>two</u> friends can't say they've made any money yet. (Neither of)
   ____
6. <u>All</u> their enthusiasm hasn't been lost, though. (None of)
   ____
7. After all, <u>it's not possible that a</u> business can be an immediate success. (No)
   ____

About you

C Answer *A*'s questions in Exercise A with information that is true for you.

1. ______________________________
2. ______________________________
3. ______________________________

Lesson B Grammar Adding information

A Is the *-ing* form in each sentence a reduced relative clause (RC), an event that happens at the same time (ST), or the subject (S) or object (O) of a verb? Write RC, ST, S, or O.

1. I enjoyed my time in high school, studying lots of different subjects. ____
2. I'll never forget walking out of my last high school class. ____
3. I left that class with tears in my eyes, feeling sad that it was all over. ____
4. I have so many friends trying to find jobs with high salaries. ____
5. But my philosophy is that making a lot of money isn't everything. ____
6. Some of the people I know working in banks are miserable. ____

B Use an *-ing* form to rewrite the underlined part of each sentence in these anecdotes.

My happiest moment in life so far . . .

1. MICHAEL: Probably my happiest moment was <u>when I got</u> my grades for my last year of college. I remember <u>that I watched</u> the mail carrier as he walked toward our mailbox. I ran outside and got the mail from him, and stood there with the envelope in my hand <u>and didn't dare</u> to open it. Eventually, I did open it <u>and I was trembling</u>. I read the page twice <u>and didn't believe</u> my eyes: straight A's. I was so happy because I knew that there would be so many opportunities <u>that were opening up</u> for me. And also <u>the fact that I got</u> straight A's showed my parents that I'd really made the most of college – they were so proud.

2. JACKY: Mine is <u>when I brought</u> home my first baby from the hospital. The people <u>who lived</u> next door came over to the house with balloons and cookies to celebrate. There are hundreds of photos of us all <u>as we drank</u> coffee and <u>ate</u> cookies. There's also a photo of each person <u>who held</u> the baby. My brother and his wife had been in the apartment for a few days <u>and had fixed up</u> the baby's room for us. They were a big help <u>and took</u> turns with the chores and everything.

3. LEE: My happiest moment is <u>the time I went</u> on vacation when I was eight. My parents looked so happy <u>as they walked</u> along the beach <u>and held</u> hands. My sister and I ran ahead, <u>and tried</u> to be the first one to get to the man <u>who sold</u> ice cream. My sister let me win, <u>and pretended</u> to get tired before we reached the truck. Then we sat on the sand <u>and ate</u> these big ice creams with chocolate sprinkles <u>and looked for</u> "white horses" in the ocean waves. Magical.

1. Probably my happiest moment was getting my grades . . .

About you

C Write an anecdote about a happy moment in your life. Use *-ing* forms.

____

____

____

____

Lesson C Conversation strategies

A Complete *B*'s answers using the words in parentheses and any expression in the box. (Use *in terms of* only once.) Then write your own answers to the questions.

as far as . . . goes / go	as far as . . . is / are concerned	in terms of	when it comes to

1. *A* What is happiness?
   B I think you can define happiness ________________ . (having no worries)
2. *A* What makes you happy?
   B ________________ , happiness is just being home with my family. (my everyday life)
3. *A* Why do people think money will make them happy?
   B I don't know. ________________ , you don't need money. (being happy)
4. *A* Do you think you can teach yourself how to be happy?
   B I guess so. Though ________________ , it's not easy for some people. (learning how to be happy)

About you

B Match the questions and answers. Write the letters a–e in the boxes. Then write your own answers using the expressions *as far as I'm concerned, as far as I can tell,* and *as far as I know*.

1. Are you generally a positive person? ☐ ________________
2. Are your friends happy? ☐ ________________
3. Do you think working in a great job makes people happy? ☐ ________________
4. Have you ever been really unhappy? ☐ ________________
5. What kinds of things make people most unhappy, do you think? ☐ ________________

a. As far as I can tell, it's relationship issues, mostly, like breakups.
b. Not really. As far as I'm concerned, life's too short. You just have to be positive about things.
c. I guess. Well, as far as I know, people say that I'm a fun guy to be around.
d. It depends. As far as I'm concerned, that's not a big deal for me, but for my friends, it is.
e. As far as I can tell, they are.

C Circle the correct options. Then complete each conversation with a correct expression in the box.

as far as I can tell	as far as I know	as far as I'm concerned

1. *A* Do you think Jerry and his fiancée will be happy? They haven't known each other long.
   B I don't know. When it comes to **divorce** / **settling down**, it's hard to know. I mean, he hasn't even met her family yet.
   A Actually, ________________ , she doesn't have any close family.
2. *A* We had the best time last year, exploring the island. Everyone's so happy there.
   B Well, it is beautiful, and as far as **lifestyle** / **work** goes, it's perfect. No stress. Nice weather.
   A Yeah, ________________ , I could happily move there tomorrow!
3. *A* So, how are things going? You seem to have a lot going on.
   B Yeah, as far as my **job** / **home life** is concerned, I'm not really enjoying it. You know, just in terms of the **type** / **amount** of work. I mean, I'm at my desk, working till ten every night.
   And ________________ , my boss doesn't appreciate it.

Lesson D Reading What is happiness?

A Prepare **Which of the following factors do you think are most important in determining a person's happiness? Check (✓) six factors.**

☐ age	☐ education	☐ family	☐ income	☐ looks	☐ religious beliefs
☐ attitude	☐ expectations	☐ friends	☐ job satisfaction	☐ marriage	☐ wealth

B Read for main ideas **Read the article. Which factors in Exercise A are most important, according to the article? Which are less important?**

What makes people HAPPY?

1 Do you know what makes you happy? People often think money is the key to happiness. While it is true that wealthy populations are happier than poor ones, seeking wealth is rarely the answer for individuals, according to many experts. In fact, once the basic needs, such as home, food, clothing, etc., are met, people in wealthier nations are only slightly happier when their incomes improve. Even lottery winners do not experience greater happiness after the thrill of winning has faded.

2 If not wealth, then what does make us happy? Most experts agree there are multiple factors contributing to happiness. Surprisingly, the research suggests that income, age, good looks, and education are only weakly linked to happiness, whereas internal factors, such as personality and attitude, hold the strongest links. Expectation plays a huge role, too. Take Denmark, for instance; although it is ranked the happiest nation in the world, its inhabitants report low expectations, according to some studies. On the other hand, people in the U.S. have higher expectations but lower levels of happiness than the Danes.

3 The evidence also suggests that happiness is, to some extent, relative. For example, in one study, college students were asked to choose between a world in which they earned $50,000 a year but everyone else earned $25,000 on average, and a world in which they earned $100,000 a year, while others earned an average of $250,000. The majority voted for the first world, because they were willing to have less, provided they were in a better position compared to others.

4 Perhaps some people are born happier than others. Studies indicate that identical twins have similar levels of happiness, and even twins separated at birth turn out equally happy. Some researchers claim there is a "set level" of happiness we are born with and that we automatically come back to. On the other hand, experts agree that people can do a lot to control their own well-being, despite their inborn characteristics.

5 Not surprisingly, friendship, family, and social networks appear to boost levels of happiness. In another study of college students, the happiest 10 percent reported strong ties with friends and family. Furthermore, those students had the lowest levels of depression. Religious faith is also frequently linked with happiness, although researchers are not sure why. Perhaps it is because of participation in strong social networks, common among religious people. Marriage and a sense of purpose at work are directly linked with happiness as well. In fact, two major events leading to depression are the loss of a spouse and the loss of a job, according to researchers. All of these factors can be important contributors to happiness or unhappiness.

6 Should political leaders then support policies meant to increase their citizens' happiness? Certainly the eradication of poverty is an important goal for all governments to pursue. Moreover, wars bring about the greatest misery, so peace may be one of the most important priorities. However, there is controversy about how much governments can actually do to stimulate happiness.

7 When it comes to happiness, many factors are involved, yet the ingredient that stands out most is expectation. People with low expectations are pleasantly surprised when things turn out better than they had thought. This doesn't mean pessimism or lack of goals will lead to happiness, but realistic expectations just might. As the saying goes, "If you expect the worst, you won't be disappointed."

C Read for detail Read the article again. Are the sentences true or false? Write T or F. Then correct the false sentences.

1. Overall, people in wealthy countries are ~~less happy~~ happier than people in poor nations. F
2. Being good-looking makes you happier than other people. ______
3. People are happier when they think their situation is better than other people's. ______
4. You can't do anything to change the level of happiness you were born with. ______
5. Religious people may have high levels of happiness because they have good jobs. ______
6. Researchers say losing a job or losing your home can lead to serious depression. ______
7. People with low expectations are often the happiest. ______

D Focus on vocabulary Find each underlined word in the article, and circle the correct synonym. Then answer the questions with your own information.

1. What makes the <u>population</u> of a country happy? (para. 1)
   a. government b. workers c. people
2. Do you know any people who <u>seek</u> wealth rather than happiness? (para. 1)
   a. try to find b. can't find c. reject
3. How can people make themselves <u>wealthier</u>? (para. 1)
   a. richer b. happier c. more satisfied
4. Do you think your <u>nation</u> is generally happy? Why or why not? (para. 2)
   a. country b. city c. continent
5. What problems might there be if there were too many <u>inhabitants</u> in a country? (para. 2)
   a. rules b. houses c. people
6. What other things should governments <u>analyze</u> – apart from economic trends? (para. 5)
   a. study b. reject c. accept
7. Should employers have <u>policies</u> for keeping workers happy? (para. 6)
   a. benefits b. plans c. culture
8. Are most of your country's <u>citizens</u> well-educated? (para. 6)
   a. people b. politicians c. teenagers
9. What are the <u>priorities</u> in your life? Wealth? Family? Happiness? (para. 6)
   a. important things b. best things c. unimportant things
10. How can the government <u>stimulate</u> the economy to grow? (para. 6)
    a. allow b. encourage c. expect

About you

E React Answer the questions with information that is true for you.

1. Which facts in the article surprised you? Which ones didn't?
   ____
2. Think of someone you know who always seems happy. Why do you think that is?
   ____
3. What do you think you can do to be happier?
   ____

Writing A paragraph in an essay

A Circle the correct options to complete the paragraph from an essay.

Why should people be more involved in their community?

There are a number of reasons why people should become more involved in community activities. Research shows there are benefits for the community **in addition / as well as** individuals. In terms of the individual, some social psychologists claim that getting involved in your community improves your satisfaction with life **in addition to / furthermore** boosting your levels of happiness. **Moreover, / As well as** the movement Action for Happiness lists connecting with people **and / moreover** doing things for your community as two of the keys to personal happiness. For these reasons alone, community involvement is positive for all residents. Community activities help to build social cohesion, contributing to a sense of well-being. **Furthermore, / In addition to** by taking a positive approach to problems such as graffiti or vandalism, people can also improve their physical environment. In conclusion, each person in a community should be involved in its activities.

B Rewrite the sentences, replacing the words in bold with the expressions given in parentheses. Make any necessary changes to the word order, grammar, or punctuation.

1. It is important to tell people about the good things going on in a community **and** its problems. (as well as) ________________
2. A community newsletter can advertise local events **and** inform people about local news. (in addition to) ________________
3. A website might **also** encourage the younger members of the community to be more involved. (Moreover) ________________
4. As far as litter is concerned, having cleanup days can be fun **and also** effective. (as well as) ________________
5. **Also**, people are less likely to litter in places that are already clean. (Furthermore) ________________
6. Holding special events can create a stronger community **and** make the neighborhood a nicer place to live. (in addition to) ________________

C Editing Correct the mistakes in these sentences. One sentence is correct.

1. Neighborhood activities benefit the community as well as makes the volunteers happy.
2. As well as provide practical help, community activities contribute to social cohesion.
3. Moreover, some communities organize events for families as well as older people to create a sense of belonging.
4. In addition to encourage volunteering, some high schools offer credits for community work.
5. Picking up trash gives volunteers a sense of satisfaction in addition discouraging them from littering the streets.
6. In addition to, cleanup days create a more pleasant environment.

D Write a paragraph to answer the essay question in Exercise A. Use at least two of the expressions in Exercise A to add ideas to your paragraph. Then check your paragraph for errors.

Listening extra Does happiness lead to success?

A Match the two parts of each sentence. Write the letters a–d. Then check (✔) the sentences you agree with.

- ☐ 1. Happiness leads to ____
- ☐ 2. Providing good education and health programs results in ____
- ☐ 3. It is true that ____
- ☐ 4. Being successful helps you avoid ____

a. being happy makes you healthier.
b. success.
c. poor health.
d. happier citizens.

B Listen to two students talk about a lecture. Check (✔) the correct answers to the questions.

1. What do the two students talk about?
   - ☐ a. The content of a lecture they attended
   - ☐ b. The length of the lecture
2. What kind of conversation do they have?
   - ☐ a. It's a friendly discussion, sharing different ideas.
   - ☐ b. It's an argument, and they're trying to make each other see a different point of view.
3. What topic do they move on to at the end of their conversation?
   - ☐ a. Their professor's health issues
   - ☐ b. Programs that can help make the citizens of a country happy

C Listen again. Circle the correct option to complete each sentence.

1. Rob's grandparents were successful as far as their **work / family life** was concerned.
2. Laurie suggests that, as far as she is concerned, work is less important than having **a nice lifestyle / close relationships**.
3. Rob read research from a university that said **happy / educated** people become successful.
4. The research also suggested that positive people don't **work / get sick** as much.
5. Laurie thinks the research **makes sense / doesn't make sense**.
6. In his lecture, Professor Blake **talked / didn't talk** about the things a country can do to make its citizens happy.

About you

D Listen again to the conversation. How would you respond? Complete the sentences with your own ideas.

1. Well, as far as I'm concerned, ____

____

____

2. As far as I can tell, ____

____

____

3. Well, when it comes to ____

____

____

Now complete the *Unit 9 Progress chart* on page 100.

Unit 10

Going places

Lesson A Vocabulary Describing travel experiences

A Circle the correct adjectives to complete the conversation.

an anaconda

A Your trip to the Amazon sounds really **fascinated / fascinating**.

B It was! The wildlife was just **amazed / amazing** – we saw monkeys, and pink dolphins, and snakes.

A Weren't you, well, **frightened / frightening** at all? I mean, I read that the Amazon has some **frightened / frightening** animals, like those huge snakes. What do you call them?

B Anacondas. Yeah, to be honest, I was **terrified / terrifying** when the guide told us about them. I guess I felt a little more **encouraged / encouraging** when he said nothing had ever happened on his tours. The worst thing we heard about was the piranhas, though.

a piranha

A Yeah? Why's that?

B Well, he said they can kill you in minutes – that was the most **surprised / surprising** thing for me.

A Really? It all sounds totally **terrified / terrifying**. But anyway, were you canoeing?

B Well, we canoed a couple of days. Though I have to say with the heat and humidity, it was pretty **challenged / challenging**.

A I bet. I'm just really **impressed / impressive** you went canoeing at all. It must have been **exhausted / exhausting**.

B Yeah. Kind of. With the change in climate, it was pretty **tired / tiring**. But it was fun.

B Complete the blog post with a correct adjective form of the verbs given.

BLOG | HOTELS | RENTALS | TOURS

My friend and I decided we wanted to go on a challenging (challenge) adventure this year, and to make a long story short, we ended up in Ecuador! After arriving in the capital city, Quito, we took a small plane into the rain forest. It was only a 16-seater, and since I'd never traveled in such a small plane before, I was far from ________ (relax). In fact, I was ________ (terrify)! The landing was bumpy, but after such a long and ________ (tire) day, I was just happy to be on solid ground. We had a light dinner at the camp, and crawled into our sleeping bags just after it got dark. However, in spite of being ________ (exhaust), I didn't sleep very well. I guess I was overtired. The next day, we got up early and started our river trip in a canoe. It was the rainy season, so I thought it was ________ (surprise) to see so many animals and birds. I told the guide I was a bit ________ (puzzle) because I hadn't expected to see so much wildlife. He explained that the animals in the forest are very active during rainy season because more food is available to them. We learned so many ________ (fascinate) things and had such a great time. I think I'm going to be feeling a bit ________ (depress) going back to work.

Lesson A Grammar Reporting what people say

A Two friends went on a hike last month. Complete the sentences with reported speech. Add *him* or *them* where necessary.

1. "We want to go hiking in the national park."
   Mike said they wanted to go hiking in the national park.
2. "There may be a storm later today. You should be prepared."
   The park ranger informed ________ . He also said ________ .
3. "I have a map, and we won't go too far."
   Mike said ________ and that ________ .
4. "We're just going for a short hike. We plan to do a longer hike tomorrow."
   Luci explained ________ . She also told ________ .
5. "You must stay on the trails or you could get lost."
   The park ranger told ________ .
6. "Some areas are dangerous because they've gotten very wet recently."
   The park ranger also explained ________ .
7. "We know the park well." "We used to hike here a lot in college."
   Luci and Mike said ________ . Mike said ________ .
8. "You can always take shelter in the huts along the trails."
   The park ranger told ________ .

B Complete the anecdote with a correct form of the verbs given. Add an indirect object pronoun (*me, him*) or no indirect object pronoun (-) after the reporting verbs *said, told,* and *explained.*

When I decided to go to Bogotá, Colombia, my friend Joaquín gave me plenty of tips about where to go, what to see, etc. Joaquín told me that I had to (have to) visit the cathedral. He said – no one ________ (should) leave the city without seeing it. He also told ____ about the Iglesia de San Francisco. He explained ____ that it ________ (be) the city's oldest church and that I ________ (will) find it amazing. Joaquín knows I love museums, so he said ____ he ________ (can) recommend a few for me to see. He said ____ that he ________ (think) that I ________ (might) like the Gold Museum and the Archaeological Museum. I told ____ that one place I ________ (look forward to) visiting ________ (be) the Botero Donation. Joaquín explained ____ that Botero, a well-known Colombian artist, ________ (donate) over 100 pieces of art to his country in the year 2000 and that they ________ (can) be found on exhibit in Bogotá. I told ____ that I ________ (must) see that.

About you

C Think of a conversation you had recently with someone before you went on a trip or simply went shopping. Report three things you said or the other person said to you. Use *said, told,* and *explained.*

My roommate and I went shopping last weekend. He said it would rain and that . . .

1. ________
2. ________
3. ________

Lesson B **Grammar** Reporting questions/instructions

A **Paulo has just arrived in New York and is telling a co-worker about his flight. Complete the sentences with the reported speech. Sometimes more than one answer is possible.**

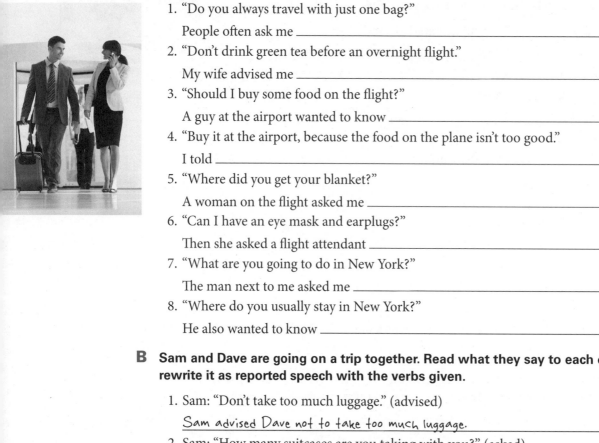

1. "Do you always travel with just one bag?"
   People often ask me ______________________________.
2. "Don't drink green tea before an overnight flight."
   My wife advised me ______________________________.
3. "Should I buy some food on the flight?"
   A guy at the airport wanted to know ______________________________.
4. "Buy it at the airport, because the food on the plane isn't too good."
   I told ______________________________.
5. "Where did you get your blanket?"
   A woman on the flight asked me ______________________________.
6. "Can I have an eye mask and earplugs?"
   Then she asked a flight attendant ______________________________.
7. "What are you going to do in New York?"
   The man next to me asked me ______________________________.
8. "Where do you usually stay in New York?"
   He also wanted to know ______________________________.

B **Sam and Dave are going on a trip together. Read what they say to each other, and rewrite it as reported speech with the verbs given.**

1. Sam: "Don't take too much luggage." (advised)
   Sam advised Dave not to take too much luggage.
2. Sam: "How many suitcases are you taking with you?" (asked)
   ____
3. Dave: "Are you taking shampoo and conditioner with you?" (wanted to know)
   ____
4. Dave: "Can you lend me a jacket for the trip?" (asked)
   ____
5. Sam: "What kind of car do you want to rent?" (asked)
   ____
6. Dave: "Make a copy of your passport." (advised)
   ____

About you

C **Complete four things you could ask a frequent traveler (1–4). Then complete two pieces of advice to travelers in your country (5–6).**

1. I'd like to know if ______________________________.
2. Can you tell me how ______________________________?
3. Can I ask you where ______________________________?
4. I've always wanted to know what ______________________________.
5. I'd advise all travelers to this country ______________________________.
6. I'd also advise them not ______________________________.

Lesson C Conversation strategies

A **Circle the correct option to complete the conversations.**

1. *A* You know, white-water rafting is not really my thing. Those rafts turn over all the time.
   B **So you mean it's perfectly safe? / So you're saying that it's too dangerous?**

2. *A* Have you ever gone skydiving?
   B Skydiving? No way! I mean, what if your parachute didn't open?
   A **So I guess you don't want to go on Saturday, then? / So you're saying it's fun?**

3. *A* You know, I've never wanted to try ski jumping. Imagine flying through the air at that height.
   B **So what you're saying is you're scared of heights? / So you mean you'd try it?**

4. *A* Come on. Let's go on the roller coaster. There are only a couple of people in line.
   B No. It doesn't look very exciting.
   A **So I guess it's not scary enough for you. / So you're saying you'll try anything?**

B **Complete the conversations with . . . *in what way?***

1. *A* I think bungee jumping is really dangerous.
   B ________________________ I mean, they check the ropes after every jump.
   A Yeah, but I think I'd rather keep my feet on the ground.

2. *A* I would love to go into space. It would be so cool!
   B ________________________ Don't you think it would be kind of scary?
   A Not really. I just think it would be exciting.

3. *A* Traveling can be life-changing.
   B ________________________
   A Well, getting to know a different culture and stuff. It changes you.

C **Complete the conversation with the appropriate follow-up questions in the box.**

a. Challenging in what way?
b. So I guess you won't be interested in doing something with me this weekend, then?
c. So you're saying that a world trip isn't exciting enough for you?
d. So you're saying you'll come?
e. You mean, like take a trip around the world or something?

Alex Wouldn't you just love to go on the trip of a lifetime someday?
Sofia ________________________
Alex No. I was actually thinking about something more challenging.
Sofia ________________________
Alex Well, I meant something really exciting – like a trip into space.
Sofia ________________________
Alex Right. I just think that seeing the world from space would be amazing – the silence, being weightless, and all that. I mean, I just want to do something really different and exciting.
Sofia ________________________ I was thinking of going mountain biking.
Alex Actually, that would be fun! Why not?
Sofia ________________________
Alex Sure. I'd love to.

Lesson D Reading Independent travel

A Prepare **What are the advantages and disadvantages of guidebooks for travelers? Write as many ideas as you can think of.**

B Read for main ideas **Find two advantages and two disadvantages of guidebooks that the writer gives. Which of your ideas were mentioned?**

Travel guides: blessing or curse?

1 If you've ever planned a trip overseas, you will probably have turned to a guidebook series in your search for information about your chosen destination. There are now dozens of guides available, but this wasn't always the case. The publication of modern guidebooks for travelers on a budget started in the 1970s as independent travel became more popular, especially among young people. There was a clear need for guides that helped independent travelers find their way in unfamiliar or exotic places and that gave honest reviews about places to stay and things to see. One or two enterprising companies answered that need. Then, over the next 30 years, guidebook publishing became a huge business and the range of countries that the books covered expanded quickly. Tony Wheeler, co-founder of one guidebook series, said that ". . . the travel book explosion was led by travelers who got into publishing rather than publishers getting into travel." In other words, the information in these types of travel guides is written by travelers for other travelers and gives insights into destinations that guidebooks had not previously provided.

2 Despite their many advantages to the independent traveler, travel guides may well have a downside, however. It's true that they encourage people to explore new places and be more adventurous; travelers, after all, don't think of themselves as tourists. However, their "insider" tips have long since become mass knowledge, available to everyone. Nowadays, no matter where you are in the world and no matter how remote the destination, you are unlikely to be alone. The chances are that when you look around, you'll see other travelers with a travel guide in their hands. A handful of independent travelers can soon turn into mass tourism as the word about a place gets around.

3 Indeed, one of the biggest threats to once quiet and remote areas – destinations that were not previously on the usual tourist trail – is an ever-increasing number of visitors. Additional tourists can adversely affect once beautiful and peaceful places. They often generate huge amounts of waste, consume resources like water and energy, and may cause problems with already struggling local infrastructures. Furthermore, the development of tourist facilities to cope with a flood of tourists can irreversibly change the traditional culture of a destination.

4 A further effect of travel guides is that people working in the industries related to tourism rely heavily on positive reviews to bring them customers. It may well be that this is good for tourists because it forces up general standards, but what are the effects on businesses that are not mentioned (perhaps because the reviewer didn't go there, or because they were set up after the guide was published, etc.)? A restaurant, store, or hotel could be excellent, but it might not get enough foreign visitors simply because it's not mentioned in the popular guides. If it's not in the guidebook, it doesn't really exist.

5 In spite of these problems, one could argue that the main value of guidebooks is that they create a better awareness among travelers of the country they are visiting. These books go further than offering tips on places to stay, eat, visit, and shop; they include information about the culture, history, and politics of an area, helping their readers to be more knowledgeable about their host country, even though this knowledge can be limited and superficial. In addition, the arrival of independent travelers (the main market for these guidebooks) can sometimes bring badly needed revenue to communities as it develops a tourist industry that employs local people to work in hotels and restaurants and at tourist sites.

6 Nevertheless, while some argue that this kind of tourism can benefit communities, the challenge for all is to manage its negative effects. The responsibility will inevitably rest on host countries, through preserving the local culture and protecting the environment. However, there is a responsibility on travelers too and guidebooks can and should make a contribution to this effort by making their readers sensitive to the issues that travel raises.

C Check your understanding **Choose the correct option to complete the sentences.**

1. Before the 1970s, the writer claims there were _____ guidebooks than there are now.
   a. fewer b. more c. better d. clearer
2. The guidebooks that were published in the 1970s became popular because they were written by people who knew about _____ .
   a. publishing b. business c. destinations d. writing
3. The writer believes that more recent guidebooks encourage independent travelers to go to places that _____ .
   a. have no tourists b. are full of tourists c. used to have no tourists d. want more tourism
4. One problem with tourism that the writer does not mention is _____ .
   a. greater energy use b. garbage or trash c. air pollution d. impact on local services
5. Some people think that guidebooks have a/an _____ value for travelers.
   a. educational b. economic c. organizational d. political
6. The writer concludes that it is the responsibility of _____ to reduce the negative effects of tourism.
   a. guidebooks b. travelers c. everyone d. host communities
7. Overall, the writer has a/an _____ view of guidebooks and tourism.
   a. negative b. positive c. balanced d. optimistic

D Understanding inference **Check (✔) the statements that the writer suggests are true.**

☐ 1. Guidebooks that were published in the 1970s were only for young people.
☐ 2. These guidebooks included information that no one had published before.
☐ 3. Independent travelers are not typical tourists.
☐ 4. Guidebooks can contribute to making quiet places into tourist destinations.
☐ 5. Real travelers will look for restaurants that are not in guidebooks.
☐ 6. A guidebook really helps you get to know a country well.

E Focus on vocabulary **Find the words in the article that are synonyms for the words in bold. Rewrite the sentences, using the synonyms.**

1. An increase in the number of tourists can **have a negative impact on** an area. (para. 3)
   An increase in the number of tourists can adversely affect an area.
2. Tourists often **produce a lot of trash** in the areas they visit. (para. 3)
   ____
3. The arrival of more tourists often means the **building** of more tourist facilities. (para. 3)
   ____
4. Reviews are beneficial to tourists because they raise standards in **businesses** that are connected with tourism. (para. 4)
   ____
5. Hotel and restaurant owners in tourist areas **are extremely dependent** on good reviews to attract foreign visitors. (para. 4)
   ____
6. Guidebooks help tourists to develop a better **understanding** of the country they are visiting. (para. 5)
   ____
7. The **income** that tourists bring can be helpful to local communities. (para. 5)
   ____
8. The tourist industry **hires** people from the local area to work in tourist facilities. (para. 5)
   ____

Writing A survey article

Survey question

Reviews of cities, restaurants, hotels, and attractions are readily available on travel websites. However, are reviews useful and would you use them before planning a trip? Why or why not?

A **Ask your friends and family the survey question above, and take notes on their views.**

B **Read the two extracts from a survey article in a student magazine. Circle the expressions in the extracts that contrast ideas.**

Are reviews useful?

• *Reviews are useless!*

Reviews on travel websites are increasingly popular, but I wanted to find out whether travelers thought they were useful. My survey shows that most people tend to read travel websites. However, they have mixed feelings about them. Although reviews can be fun or interesting, many people said that the information in them is not always up to date. In fact, most people said they ignore reviews despite the useful information that they might contain. A receptionist in a hotel said . . .

• *Reviews are useful!*

Online reviews are said to make traveling easier. I asked some tourists whether they thought reviews were worth reading. Interestingly enough, even though many travelers think that reviews are not always accurate, most say that the advantages outweigh the disadvantages. It is true that any review is only the personal opinion of one person. Nevertheless, most people think that without reviews, it would be more difficult to plan a vacation. We need reviews in spite of their limitations.

C **Editing** **Correct the mistakes in these sentences from survey articles. Change the expression in bold, or the punctuation, or both. Sometimes more than one answer is possible.**

1. **In spite of** reviews are opinions, they are a useful source of information.
   Although/Even though reviews are opinions, they are a useful source of information.
2. **Despite** reviews make restaurants busier, they ensure that general standards improve.
3. Reviews are a good thing **although** the problems that they may cause.
4. Reviews might not always be up to date. **Even though** travelers generally like to read them.
5. **Although** the disadvantages of tourism in remote areas, there are benefits such as employment.
6. Most people still enjoy their vacations **although** the crowds of tourists in some resorts.

D **Write an article to answer the survey question. Give examples of the things your friends or family said. Then check your article for errors.**

Listening extra An eco-tour

A Eco-tourism is traveling in a responsible way, which doesn't harm the environment. What words and expressions would you expect to hear in a conversation about an eco-tour? Write four more ideas.

amazing rain forest relaxing wildlife

__________ __________ __________ __________

B Listen to the conversation. Check (✔) the best sentence to complete the summary of the speaker's views.

Rick believes that the countries he visited . . .

☐ a. don't do anything to protect the local environment.
☐ b. benefit greatly from eco-tourism.
☐ c. should develop their eco-tourism industries.

C Listen again. Are the sentences true or false? Write T or F. Correct the false sentences.

1. Rick said that he was tired of beach vacations. ____
2. He told Haley that he enjoyed the eco-tour, but the places they stayed weren't very impressive. ____
3. Haley asked whether eco-tourism had a negative impact on the environment. ____
4. Rick explained that monkeys were still afraid of the tourists. ____
5. Rick said they had used local transportation and restaurants. ____
6. Rick thinks eco-tourism is a positive thing overall. ____

D Listen again and complete the sentences with the missing numbers.

1. Rick said one of the places they visited got over __________ tourists each year.
2. Rick's tour guide said that tourist numbers had increased by __________ percent in recent years.
3. The guide also mentioned that one of the national parks had up to __________ visitors each day.
4. Rick said he had paid a $__________ entrance fee at one of the nature reserves.
5. The country that Rick visited earns over $__________ in revenue from producing coffee.

About you

E Listen again to the last part of the conversation. What advantages of eco-tourism does Rick mention? Write notes. Do you agree with him? Write your response below.

1. __________
2. __________
3. __________

Your response:

____

____

____

Now complete the *Unit 10 Progress chart* on page 101.

Unit 11

Culture

Lesson A Vocabulary Describing wedding customs

A Match the definitions with the words. Write the letters a–h.

1. This person finds someone a partner. ____
2. This man has just gotten married. ____
3. This woman has just gotten married. ____
4. This man helps the groom. ____
5. These women help the bride. ____
6. The mother and father of the man who has just gotten married. ____
7. At a Western-style ceremony, they show guests where to sit. ____
8. The couple that has just gotten married. ____

a. best man
b. bride
c. bridesmaids
d. groom
e. groomsmen
f. matchmaker
g. newlyweds
h. parents of the groom

B Complete the sentences with the words and phrases in the box.

aisle	bachelor	civil ceremony	host	reception	Western-style
arranged	✔ bachelorette	exchange	performs	vows	

1. Before the wedding, the bride and her female friends have a bachelorette party.
2. In the same way, the groom and his male friends have a ________ party.
3. The parents of the groom ________ a dinner the evening before the wedding.
4. In some weddings – for example, ________ weddings – the bride and her father walk down the ________ .
5. During the ceremony, the bride and groom ________ rings – often simple gold or silver bands.
6. As the bride and groom give each other the rings, they exchange ________ , promising to love each other forever.
7. Some couples prefer to have a religious wedding; others prefer a ________ .
8. In some weddings, a celebrity look-alike ________ the ceremony.
9. After the wedding, the bride and groom and the guests go to the ________ .
10. People that meet each other through a matchmaker have an ________ marriage.

About you

C Answer the questions with information about typical weddings in your country.

1. What kinds of weddings do people typically have?

____

____

2. What kinds of traditions are associated with weddings?

____

____

3. Are bachelor and bachelorette parties popular? What other traditions are there before a couple gets married?

____

____

Lesson A Grammar Adding information

A Complete the blog post with *when, where,* or *whose.* Add commas where necessary. Sometimes more than one answer is possible.

BLOG

I live in a small town ______________ everyone gets married before they're 30, so I have a lot of friends ______________ only ambition is to get married. To me this seems like a waste of your youth, which is a time ______________ you should be enjoying yourself. What's even worse is that I have some friends ______________ parents are almost forcing them to find a partner. They feel ashamed if they're still single at 30 ______________ people say they're "over the hill" – as if 30 is old! I just think this is a very old-fashioned view, especially in today's society ______________ there are so many opportunities to do other things. I think it's better to wait and get married in your thirties ______________ you know exactly what you want. I'm sure you get to a point in your life ______________ you want to settle down with one special person. I think, though, you have to make your own choices and not be persuaded by people ______________ own life choices might be different from yours.

B Rewrite each pair of sentences as one sentence, using relative clauses. Replace the words in bold with *when, where,* or *whose.* You may need to change the word order and the punctuation.

1. I'll always remember my best friend's wedding. Nothing went right **there**.

   ____

2. The day before the wedding, we had a rehearsal. **Then** everything went really well.

   ____

3. However, later that evening, the couple was late because their taxi broke down. **Their** parents hosted a really expensive dinner.

   ____

4. There was a very funny moment during the ceremony. **At this moment**, the groom got the bride's name wrong as he was saying his vows.

   ____

5. The best man left the groom's ring in his car. **His** job was to take care of the rings.

   ____

6. After the ceremony, we all got into cars to go to the hotel. The reception was being held **there**.

   ____

7. The car took me and the other bridesmaids to the wrong hotel, and we didn't realize till the very last moment. **That was the moment** we saw the car drive away.

   ____

8. For the newlyweds, the reception was the best time. **Then** everything finally went according to plan.

   ____

About you

C Complete the sentences to make them true for you. Add commas where necessary.

1. It would be nice to get married in ______________ where ______________ .
2. A lot of people get married in ______________ when ______________ .
3. If I get married, I would have a ______________ whose job would be to ______________ .

Lesson B **Grammar** Giving things to people

A Unscramble the sentences to complete the conversations.

1. *A* You know what I've just realized? I never gave you a birthday present!
   (a / gave / I / you / never / birthday present!)
   B Yes, you did. Don't you remember? ______________________ in the mail.
   (a gift card / me / You / sent)

2. *A* ______________________
   (offer / you / I / something to drink? / Can)
   B Yes, please. ______________________
   (Could / make / tea / some / you / us? / for)

3. *A* What did your brother get for his birthday? ______________________ again?
   (a / sweater / Did / for / him / make / your aunt)
   B No. ______________________ this year.
   (make / one / him / didn't / She)

4. *A* ______________________
   (Would / blue jacket? / you / me / your / lend)
   B Sure, no problem! Actually, I don't wear it much. ______________________
   (I'll / it / give / you / to / if you like.)

5. *A* ______________________ They smell wonderful.
   (flowers? / you / sent / these / Who)
   B ______________________ out of the blue.
   (them / sent / My girlfriend / to / me)

6. *A* Isn't it your parents' anniversary today? ______________________
   (Did / get / you / a gift? / them)
   B Yes, it's today. ______________________ last weekend.
   (one / them / bought / I)

About you

B Rewrite the questions using the alternate pattern where possible. Then write answers that are true for you, using the pronouns *it, them,* or *one*.

1. Would you ever lend your laptop to a friend?
   Q: Would you ever lend a friend your laptop?
   A: Yes, I'd lend it to him. OR: No, I wouldn't lend it to him.

2. When would you give money as a gift to someone?
   Q: ______________________
   A: ______________________

3. Did you buy a birthday present for your best friend last year?
   Q: ______________________
   A: ______________________

4. If a good friend liked your new, expensive pen, would you give it to him or her?
   Q: ______________________
   A: ______________________

5. When you were little, did you use to make your parents cards or gifts?
   Q: ______________________
   A: ______________________

Lesson C Conversation strategies

A Match the sentences and the responses. Write the letters a–e.

1. I never know what gifts to buy for people. ____
2. I always treat myself to something a bit special on my birthday, like a new outfit or something. ____
3. You know, I never buy birthday cards. There isn't really any point – no one keeps them. ____
4. You know what I hate? They always put seasonal gifts out in the stores months ahead. ____
5. We never wrap gifts. Do you? We just put something in a gift bag. It's so much easier. ____

a. Though kids like to open all the paper and ribbons, and stuff. It's kind of more fun for them.
b. Right. Though it's slightly odd not to get a card. You can always send an e-card, I guess.
c. Which is sort of nice – to spend money on yourself occasionally.
d. I know. I find it kind of difficult to choose the right thing, too.
e. I know. It's not quite right. I'd rather buy stuff a couple of weeks before the actual holiday.

B Check (✓) the appropriate response in each conversation.

1. *A* I think it's kind of fun to share our traditions with people from other cultures.
   B ☐ Yeah, no. It's kind of important for everyone to know about other customs.
   ☐ Yeah, no. There's no point in learning about other cultures.
2. *A* I've gotten birthday punches ever since I was a kid. I sort of look forward to them.
   B ☐ Yeah, no. It's not very nice. I mean, I'd be somewhat upset, too.
   ☐ Yeah, no. It's good to carry on traditions like that – even if they are slightly odd!
3. *A* Traveling teaches you a lot about different cultures. I think everyone should travel more.
   B ☐ Yeah, no. It helps you understand other people, which makes you more tolerant, I think.
   ☐ Yeah, no. It doesn't really educate you at all.

About you

C Complete *A*'s comments with softening expressions. Use at least five different expressions. Then write your own responses to complete the conversations. If you agree, use *Yeah, no*.

1. *A* Why do we celebrate birthdays anyway? In some societies, they don't celebrate birthdays. I mean, they think it's ____________ odd. They just celebrate when you achieve something in your life, which is ____________ interesting.
   You: ____
2. *A* I hate it when people send me e-cards. I don't know. It just seems ____________ right. I mean, ____________ lazy – like you don't ____________ want to make the effort to get me a real card.
   You: ____
3. *A* I think it's ____________ important when you get married to start your own traditions together. It makes your relationship stronger.
   You: ____
4. *A* I always think it's ____________ weird – how people celebrate all the different holidays. I mean, even if they don't believe in them. It's just ____________ strange, you know? Like, it's just an excuse to buy presents and stuff.
   You: ____

Lesson D **Reading** Reverse culture shock

A Prepare **What do you think reverse culture shock is? Check (✓) one box below. Then read the article. Was your answer correct?**

☐ It's what happens when you visit another culture and very little surprises you.
☐ It's the difficulty adjusting to your own culture after living in another one.
☐ It's the problems you have when you first experience a different culture.

Are you ready for reverse culture shock?

1 The term *culture shock*, is used to describe the feeling of unease and/or loss you might experience when visiting or living in a country that is not your own. You might have problems being in a place where you don't speak the language and everyday life is quite different from what you're used to. Initially, this reaction – this shock – may be caused by the feeling that the foreign culture is a threat to your own culture and identity.

2 Less well known, however, is the term *reverse culture shock*, which refers to the difficulties someone can experience on the return to their native country after living abroad. Most people accept that culture shock is a normal part of being in a foreign country. However, it is not so widely understood that people coming home after a stay abroad might also experience a similar kind of culture shock. Living in another country changes you: once you're home, you're no longer the same person who left. With global travel becoming more and more popular and more people living abroad for longer periods of time, it is difficult to dismiss reverse culture shock as something that only happens to a handful of people. It is clearly becoming a more common problem.

3 The level of reverse culture shock that people experience varies, depending on factors such as how positive their experience abroad was and how different the other culture was from their own. It is, however, perfectly normal, and is usually experienced in distinct phases.

4 **PHASE 1** You've made the decision to go home after a few months, years, or decades abroad. It is no less of a big step to take than the decision that brought you to the foreign country in the first place. This time you're leaving a country whose culture you worked hard to understand, where you learned to communicate, and where you made a life. You're leaving a lot behind, but you're probably too excited and too busy preparing to think about that.

5 **PHASE 2** Back home again, you're happy to see friends and family, and they're happy to see you. It's almost like being in a new country, but with the added benefit of knowing the language and culture. You can revive relationships with friends and family, and tell them about your experiences. You look for the opportunity to point out how differently people do things in the other culture. In fact, that's all you seem to want to talk about – something that your friends and family might not appreciate.

6 **PHASE 3** At this point, the downside of moving back hits you. You sense that you're always focusing on the differences between your native country and the country you came from and you don't feel good about it. You might also feel that people in your native country don't really understand you. Since you're used to a different culture, you now feel somewhat uncomfortable in your own. At the same time, you want to preserve everything you feel was good about your time abroad and don't want other people or daily life in your native country to kill off those experiences and those memories. Consequently, you might feel homesick for the other country or even want to return there. This is a natural part of reverse culture shock.

7 **PHASE 4** After a few months, you'll focus less on the differences between the countries. What was once most important to you – the preservation of your old way of life in a foreign culture – will become less so. You'll feel comfortable again with your first language, and people will come to accept you, as you will also be able to accept them.

8 As you adjust, things will start to seem normal again. Try to combine the positive aspects of your international experience with the positive aspects of your life at home. Make an effort to meet people and take part in the local culture as much as possible. If you can do that, you will finally put reverse culture shock behind you.

B Read for main ideas **The article describes four phases of reverse culture shock. Write the number of the phase (1–4) next to each description. There are two extra descriptions.**

a. You'll accept the fact that you are back home. ____
b. You badly miss your friends and family. ____
c. You're happy to be going back home. ____
d. You really miss the foreign country and consider moving back. ____
e. You re-learn your first language. ____
f. You're excited to see people you love and share your experiences abroad. ____

C Check your understanding **Choose the correct option to complete the sentences.**

1. The article suggests that culture shock ______ .
   a. happens to very few people b. is a misunderstood term c. is a well-recognized experience
2. According to the article, reverse culture shock is ______ .
   a. increasing b. declining c. about the same as it always was
3. The article is most useful for people who are going to ______ .
   a. emigrate b. return home after a period abroad c. live abroad for a few months

D Read for detail **Are the sentences true or false? Write T or F. Correct the false sentences.**

1. A lot of people are familiar with the term *reverse culture shock.* ____
2. Reverse culture shock affects a small number of people. ____
3. The article describes reverse culture shock as a normal experience. ____
4. The article states that reverse culture shock can happen after a week's vacation abroad. ____
5. Friends and family might not be very understanding about the effects of reverse culture shock. ____
6. Reverse culture shock is something that people can get over. ____

E Vocabulary in context **Complete the sentences with words from the article that mean the opposite of the words and phrases in bold.**

1. After leaving a foreign culture, many people feel that its **preservation** in their lives is particularly important. They feel a sense of ________ when they move from one culture to another. (para. 1)
2. It is important to **accept** reverse culture shock as a real problem for people, but some people simply ________ it. (para. 2)
3. Reverse culture shock is not limited to being a **local** issue in one or two countries. It is becoming a ________ one. (para. 2)
4. People who return to their native country may need to ________ old friendships. However, they can soon **kill** them **off** by talking too much about their life abroad. (para. 5)
5. Some people see living in a new culture as a **threat** to their own lifestyle and values. Others see it as an ________ to assess their own culture. (para. 5)
6. Moving back home has **benefits**, but there is also a ________ . (para. 6)

About you

F React **What do you think people would have difficulty adjusting to if they came to live in your country? Give reasons for your answer.**

____

____

____

____

Writing A conclusion to an essay

Essay question

Is reverse culture shock a positive or a negative experience?

A Read the thesis statements and the concluding paragraphs. Which thesis statement was in the introduction to each essay? Write a, b, or c. There is one extra option.

a. It is not possible to say if reverse culture shock is a positive or negative experience, since that depends on the individual experiencing it.

b. Reverse culture shock is a negative experience due to the confusion it creates in a person's mind about his or her own culture.

c. Because it gives people the opportunity to develop their minds in various ways, reverse culture shock is a positive experience overall.

1. ☐ In conclusion, reverse culture shock affects people differently. Consequently, it is difficult to know exactly how the experience will affect a person. Nevertheless, the benefits of travel are great, so people should not avoid travel because of a fear of reverse culture shock.	2. ☐ In summary, although it can be challenging, reverse culture shock brings many benefits. People may become more open-minded and understand others better as a result of the experience. Therefore, instead of being afraid of reverse culture shock, we should see it as an opportunity for growth.

B Read the concluding paragraphs in Exercise A again. Circle the expressions that express causes, effects, and results.

C Complete the sentences with the expressions in the box. Sometimes more than one answer is possible.

as a result of	because	because of	consequently	due to	since	so	therefore

1. Reverse culture shock is not well understood, ________ we need to learn about it.
2. ________, there should be more information about it for migrants.
3. Our awareness of ourselves increases ________ reverse culture shock.
4. Our understanding of the world changes ________ we see things differently.
5. Reverse culture shock is positive ________ it shows that we have successfully taken on a new way of life in a different culture.
6. ________ reverse culture shock, some people might change for the better.
7. Reverse culture shock is a problem. ________, we need to help people with it.

D Editing Correct the sentences. There is one error in each sentence.

1. Your friends might get annoyed due to your complaints about your own culture.
2. I am worried about returning home from a year abroad because reverse culture shock.
3. You are going home soon, consequently start catching up on the news of your country.
4. Since reverse culture shock, I learned a lot about myself and my culture.
5. People will not stop traveling just due to their fear of getting reverse culture shock.

E Write a concluding paragraph to answer the essay question. Include two arguments to support your answer. Then check your paragraph for errors.

Listening extra A destination wedding

A **Look at the photos. What do you think a "destination wedding" is? Check (✓) a, b, or c.**

☐ a. It's a wedding where the couple has never met before, because it's been arranged by a matchmaker.

☐ b. It's a wedding that is held in a location that isn't the bride's or the groom's hometown.

☐ c. It's a civil ceremony that is performed by a government official.

B **Listen to the conversation. Was your answer in Exercise A correct? Then check (✓) the topics Diana and her friend Atsuko discuss.**

☐ Diana's new responsibilities at work
☐ A recent trip Atsuko made
☐ Atsuko's friend's wedding
☐ The health of Diana's family
☐ Buying wedding gifts
☐ The advantages of getting married close to home

C **Listen again. Circle the correct option to complete each sentence.**

1. Diana and Atsuko haven't seen each other for **a few days** / **a long time**.
2. Atsuko was **a bridesmaid** / **a guest** at her friend's wedding.
3. Diana's cousin wanted a **big** / **small** wedding.
4. Atsuko's friend had a **Western-style** / **traditional** wedding.
5. Atsuko cried at the moment when her friend **helped her father down the aisle** / **said her vows**.
6. Atsuko's only complaint was that the trip **cost a lot** / **was too short**.
7. Diana **attended** / **didn't attend** her cousin's wedding.
8. Atsuko **bought** / **didn't buy** a gift for her friend.

About you

D **Listen again to some of the comments Diana and Atsuko make. Write your own responses. Use *Yeah, no* if you agree.**

1. ______________________________
2. ______________________________
3. ______________________________
4. ______________________________

About you

E **Answer the questions. Give as much information as you can.**

1. Has anyone you know ever had a destination wedding? Are they popular in your country?
____
2. What do you think about destination weddings? Are they a good idea?
____

Now complete the *Unit 11 Progress chart* on page 99.

Unit 12

Ability

Lesson A Vocabulary Talking about intelligence

A Complete the sentences with the types of intelligence in the box.

bodily	interpersonal	intrapersonal	linguistic	mathematical	musical	spatial

1. Architects need ____________ intelligence so they can design living spaces.
2. Some people can play an instrument well. They have ____________ intelligence.
3. People who don't understand others often have no ____________ intelligence.
4. People who know themselves and what they want tend to have ____________ intelligence.
5. A lot of children have ____________ intelligence and learn through play and movement.
6. Computer programmers have ____________ intelligence. Many study math.
7. It's easy to confuse ____________ intelligence with being generally very smart. Perhaps because it's important to be able to communicate well.

B Complete the sentences with the words in the box. Sometimes more than one answer is possible.

adept	capacity	sensitive
articulate	literate	skilled
capable	scientifically minded	talent

1. My dad's so good at math. He's ____________ of solving any problem.
2. My friend really has a ____________ for music. He can play anything.
3. My brother always seems to find the right words in any situation. He's very ____________ .
4. My mom volunteers in a school, teaching kids to read. She says the key to success in life is to be ____________ .
5. I'm not at all ____________ . I have no idea about physics or chemistry or anything like that.
6. When I have a problem, I always talk to my sister. She's so ____________ to everyone's feelings. She has a great ____________ for understanding people.
7. I can't fix anything in the house if it breaks. I guess I'm just not ____________ at things like that.
8. My friend is very ____________ at balancing work and his social life. It's good to be able to do that.

About you

C Use the expressions in the box to write sentences that are true for you or people you know.

be (not very) adept at	be (in)capable of	be (not very) skilled at
be (un)able to	be (not very) efficient at	have a/no talent for

1. ____________________
2. ____________________
3. ____________________
4. ____________________
5. ____________________
6. ____________________

Lesson A Grammar Describing people and things

A **Add the adverb form of the adjectives in parentheses to these sentences. Sometimes more than one answer is possible.**

1. Singers don't have to be ^technically perfect – they just need to be able to express emotions. (technical)
2. It's important to get a college education to get ahead in life. (extreme)
3. If you are a lawyer, you need to be very articulate to become skilled. (high)
4. I don't believe that some people can speak seven languages – no one can be so gifted. (linguistic)
5. It's interesting to read about different types of minds and intelligences. (incredible)
6. Students who are very musical often do well in math, too. (remarkable)
7. Intrapersonal intelligence is difficult to learn, but it's an important skill. (particular)
8. It's easy to take really good photos with the latest cameras. (relative)

About you

B **Rewrite five of the sentences above, either giving your own views or adding more ideas.**

I think you also need to have especially good interpersonal skills to be a successful lawyer.

____

____

____

____

C **Complete the blog post with a correct adverb or adjective form of the words given.**

BLOG 24 MAY No comments

I've never really been ______________ (mathematical / talented), but I needed math to graduate from high school. So my mom contacted a friend of hers, Valli, who had been ______________ (particular / good) at math when they were in school together. Valli wasn't ______________ (high / qualified), but she was ______________ (extreme / patient) and gave me ______________ (incredible) confidence. You see, she was an elementary school teacher, so she had a ______________ (wonderful) talent for describing and explaining things ______________ (extreme / clear). She started at the beginning with ______________ (basic) principles and we went over everything ______________ (slow). I learned a lot from her ______________ (remarkable / quick), and although I still found math ______________ (relative / difficult), I managed to get a passing grade.

About you

D **Write sentences about . . .**

1. an activity you are relatively skilled at. ______________
2. a place that you think is remarkably beautiful. ______________
3. something you find physically impossible. ______________
4. a subject that you find particularly challenging. ______________
5. a piece of news you find incredibly interesting. ______________

Lesson B Grammar Comparing

A Complete the conversations with the comparative or superlative form of the adjective or adverb given. Use *less, least, more,* or *most* where necessary.

1. *A* Hey, your English is improving. I mean, you speak a lot ______________ (well) and much ______________ (confidently) than before.
   B Well, I just took an intensive course. It was ______________ (hard) thing I ever did, and I was ______________ (bad) student in the class, but it helped.
2. *A* Every time I play my flute, I think I'm playing ______________ (badly) than ever.
   B Well, maybe you need to practice ______________ (frequently).
   A I know, but finding time is ______________ (hard) thing. I'm ______________ (busy) now than I ever was.
3. *A* I hate going to discos. I think I must be just about ______________ (bad) dancer in the world. It's the one thing I feel ______________ (confident) about.
   B Well, come out with me and Katia. Maybe you'll feel ______________ (nervous).
   A Thanks. But Katia's ______________ (good) dancer I've ever seen. I think it'd make me feel ______________ (embarrassed).
4. *A* Hey, you're early! The traffic must have been ______________ (good) than usual.
   B Actually, I came on my bike. I can get across town much ______________ (quickly) than in my car. It's ______________ (easy), too. You don't need to find a parking space.
   A Right. And it keeps you in shape. You look ______________ (healthy) than ever!

B Circle the correct option to complete the blog posts.

Q & A BLOG

Q: I sometimes need to give presentations, but I'm not as **confident / confidently** as I'd like to be. Is there anything I can do so it becomes **easier / more easily**?
A: Why not take a public-speaking class? Then you'll have the chance to practice more **often / frequent**, and you'll feel **less / least** nervous. Find the best course **in / of** your area.

Q: I don't speak Spanish as well **as / than** I did when I lived in Spain. Any suggestions?
A: You need to practice **as often as / more often** you can. Joining a conversation group is the **best / better** way to get the practice you need. It's also **the least / less** expensive way.

About you

C Complete *B*'s responses. Then write answers that are true for you.

1. *A* Would you like to be more confident when you speak English?
   B Yes, I'm not as confident as I'd like to be.
2. *A* Is English the hardest class you have ever taken?
   B No, I think math is ______________________________.
3. *A* Had you hoped to improve your English more quickly?
   B Yes, I feel that I'm not improving ______________________________.
4. *A* What skill should you practice more often?
   B Probably typing. I don't ______________________________.
5. *A* What do your friends do better than you?
   B They all drive better. I'm ______________________________ of all my friends.

Lesson C Conversation strategies

A Complete the sentences. Write the letters a–g.

1. My parents bought me a piano ____ , but I still never learned to play well.
2. To succeed, it's not enough to be gifted. You have to be serious, ____ .
3. I don't think it's a good idea for parents to push their children ____ .
4. I have a lot of practical skills, like I can build furniture, ____ .
5. I wish I could write music ____ , but I'm not as creative as I'd like to be.
6. I guess I'm not a very disciplined student. I'm always turning assignments in late ____ .
7. I know this twelve-year-old girl who's amazingly gifted. She already does algebra ____ .

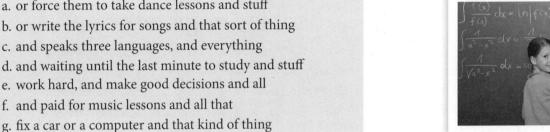

a. or force them to take dance lessons and stuff
b. or write the lyrics for songs and that sort of thing
c. and speaks three languages, and everything
d. and waiting until the last minute to study and stuff
e. work hard, and make good decisions and all
f. and paid for music lessons and all that
g. fix a car or a computer and that kind of thing

B Circle the best option to complete the conversations.

1. *A* **I think I did well on / I'm afraid I failed** my tests this week.
   B Oh, no doubt. You've done all your homework, and you studied hard, so . . .
2. *A* I think my sister **will make a great nurse / will decide not to go into nursing**.
   B I don't doubt it. She's really good at caring for other people.
3. *A* I think speaking in public is **fun / something you have to practice**.
   B Oh, there's no doubt about that. I mean, you can be articulate and all that, but still find it difficult.

C Complete the conversations with vague expressions and expressions like *No doubt*. Don't repeat any expression. Then write your own responses to *A*'s comments.

1. *A* Families don't seem to play board games anymore. You know, like chess, checkers, ________________ . It's too bad because kids learn a lot of valuable skills from games like that.
   B Oh, ________________ . They say chess is really good for teaching problem solving.
   You: ____
2. *A* All kids should do music and play an instrument ________________ . It's good for them.
   B Oh, ________________ . They say if you're good at music, you'll be good at math, too.
   You: ____
3. *A* All kids are good with technology because they grow up with computers ________________ .
   B Oh, ________________ . Yeah, no. They figure out all that stuff early on.
   You: ____
4. *A* I've heard that a lot of students in college aren't capable of producing a well-written essay.
   B ________________ . They don't focus enough on spelling and writing ________________ .
   You: ____

Lesson D **Reading** Overcoming dyslexia

A **The word *dyslexia* comes from the Greek: *dys* meaning "ill" or "difficult," and *lexis* meaning "word." Which statements do you think are true about people with dyslexia? Check (✓) the boxes.**

- ☐ They have trouble reading, writing, and spelling.
- ☐ They are lazy in school.
- ☐ They are often especially intelligent.
- ☐ They usually never learn to read.
- ☐ They are not as articulate as other people.

B Read for main ideas **Read the article. Which of the statements in Exercise A are true?**

Actors with dyslexia: disabled or gifted?

1 Dyslexia is a language-based learning disability that makes reading, writing, and spelling difficult. The experience of being dyslexic can be extremely challenging. People often have preconceived ideas about dyslexic children who cannot keep up in class or who find it difficult to spell or read properly, and they are often labeled "lazy" as a consequence. These students may feel inadequate, lose interest in studying at an early age, and even quit school. Although people with dyslexia are faced with learning challenges from an early age, many are highly intelligent and succeed in a wide range of careers. There are world-champion swimmers, and Formula One racers with dyslexia – but *actors*? Surprisingly, even though actors need to be skilled at reading scripts, as well as adept at learning lines, there are a number of well-known and highly successful actors who have this condition.

Keanu Reeves

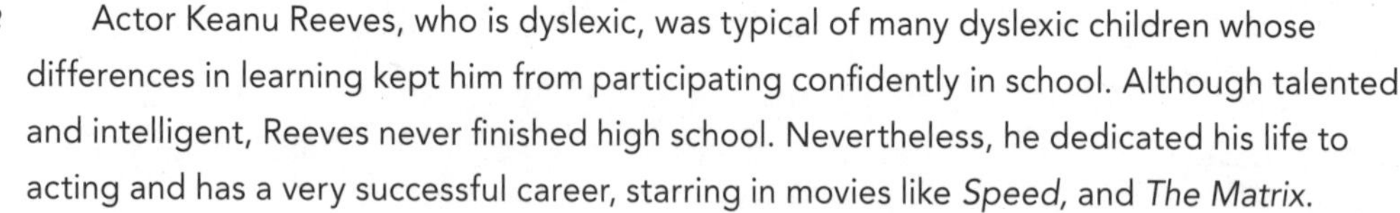

2 Actor Keanu Reeves, who is dyslexic, was typical of many dyslexic children whose differences in learning kept him from participating confidently in school. Although talented and intelligent, Reeves never finished high school. Nevertheless, he dedicated his life to acting and has a very successful career, starring in movies like *Speed*, and *The Matrix*.

Orlando Bloom

3 Actors with dyslexia often have to work harder than other actors in order to be successful. Actors have to read and remember many lines of text. While for some, remembering lines is relatively easy, others spend half their lives studying scripts. Orlando Bloom, whose movies include *Lord of the Rings* and *Pirates of the Caribbean*, has said that reading and memorizing his lines is very hard work. Actor Keira Knightley, also dyslexic, said that, when she was growing up, reading was a tremendous challenge for her but that the struggle made her tougher. The star of *Pride and Prejudice* says that she drove herself very hard to overcome dyslexia and finished school with top grades, in spite of her disability.

Keira Knightley

4 Successful actors with dyslexia challenge our views about disabilities. Conventional wisdom says that dyslexia is a disability. Today, however, some researchers believe that it is actually a natural ability, a talent. They believe that people with dyslexia, if supported and allowed to develop, have higher than normal intelligence and can be more creative. Orlando Bloom looks at dyslexia as a gift, saying that rather than being a disability, it is a challenge that he uses as motivation to have "a big life."

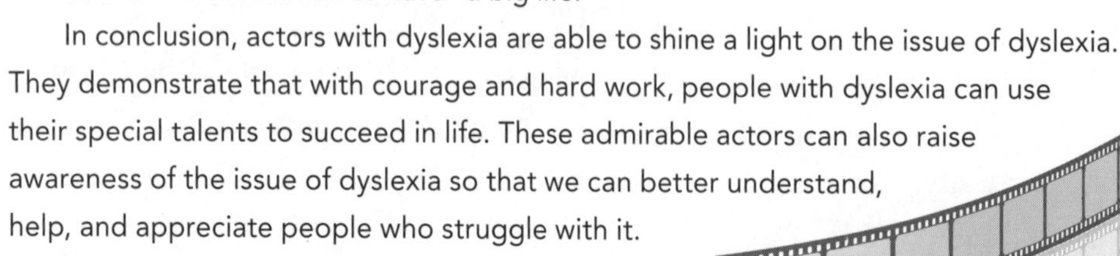

5 In conclusion, actors with dyslexia are able to shine a light on the issue of dyslexia. They demonstrate that with courage and hard work, people with dyslexia can use their special talents to succeed in life. These admirable actors can also raise awareness of the issue of dyslexia so that we can better understand, help, and appreciate people who struggle with it.

C Understanding viewpoints Would the writer of the article agree with these views? Write Y (Yes), N (No), or NG (Not Given, if it is impossible to say what the writer thinks).

1. Being dyslexic can be slightly difficult at times. ______
2. Dyslexic children have a harder time than dyslexic adults. ______
3. Dyslexic people quit school because their problems haven't been understood. ______
4. It's not surprising that dyslexic people go into acting as a career. ______
5. Keanu Reeves lacked confidence at high school. ______
6. Actors with dyslexia can easily overcome their difficulties. ______
7. Dyslexic actors are often more successful than other actors. ______
8. People generally see dyslexia as a disability. ______
9. Dyslexia doesn't have to be seen as a disability. ______
10. Actors with dyslexia spend a lot of time promoting awareness of the condition. ______

D Read for detail Circle the correct answers to the questions.

1. Why do dyslexic children sometimes feel inadequate?
   a. They quit school early.
   b. They find lessons difficult.
   c. They have too many preconceived ideas.
   d. They develop few interests.
2. In what way was Keanu Reeves typical of many dyslexic children?
   a. He wanted to be famous.
   b. He became highly successful.
   c. He didn't graduate from high school.
   d. He had a talent for acting.
3. What effect has dyslexia had on Keira Knightley?
   a. It made her difficult to work with.
   b. It made her more intelligent.
   c. It made her successful.
   d. It made her stronger.
4. How do more recent views of dyslexia differ from conventional wisdom?
   a. They see dyslexia as a positive thing.
   b. They say dyslexic people have courage.
   c. They view dyslexia as a disability.
   d. They say dyslexia gives people a better life.

E Focus on vocabulary Find the words in the article that are used with the words in bold. Then use the words to complete the sentences below.

1. People often **have** ______________ **ideas** about children who have trouble reading. (para. 1)
2. One person with dyslexia became a ______________-______________ **swimmer**. (para. 1)
3. Keanu Reeves has ______________ his **life** to his acting career. (para. 2)
4. Some actors ______________ **half** their **lives** studying scripts. (para. 3)
5. Successful actors ______________ our **views** about dyslexia. (para. 4)
6. Although ______________ **wisdom** says that dyslexia is a disability, for some it may be a talent. (para. 4)
7. Dyslexic actors ______________ **a light** on the issue of dyslexia. (para. 5)
8. Actors like Keanu Reeves, Orlando Bloom, and Keira Knightley ______________ **awareness** of the issue of dyslexia. (para. 5)

About you

F React Answer three of the questions with information that is true for you.

1. What did you know about dyslexia before you read the article?
2. Did the article affect your view of dyslexia in any way? If so, how?
3. Did the article contain any information that was new or surprising to you? If so, what?
4. Do you feel the article left any information out or got any information wrong? In what way?
5. What else would you like to know about dyslexia?

Writing An essay

Essay question

Choose three of your most important skills or abilities, and say why they are or will be important in your life. Give specific reasons and details to support your answer.

A **Read the beginning of an essay. Underline the three skills or abilities the writer mentions. Then complete the sentences with the expressions in the box.**

in order to succeed	so that I don't make	so I can understand	to be

There are three abilities and skills that are important in my life, and that I rely on ____________ happy and successful. First, I have an ability to understand other people's feelings. This is one of the main reasons I have a wide circle of friends. Second, I have excellent study skills, which are important ____________ in school and work. Third, my ability to understand myself extremely well is a critical skill to have ____________ poor choices in life. Together, I believe these three skills will enable me to achieve both success and happiness.

In terms of the first ability, I feel I have a particularly high level of interpersonal intelligence. For example, I am always sensitive to other people's feelings. I listen to people very carefully ____________ their points of view. . . .

B **Rewrite each pair of sentences as one sentence, using the expressions in parentheses. Make any other necessary changes to the original sentences.**

1. When I don't see my friends regularly, I call them. I want to keep in touch. (in order to)
   When I don't see my friends regularly, I call them in order to keep in touch.
2. I often send friends a quick text message. I want to say "good luck" before a test. (to)
   ____
3. I always keep my promises. That way people know they can trust me. (so)
   ____
4. I tend to study on weeknights. Then I have time for my friends on the weekends. (so that)
   ____
5. Every day I set aside some time. That way I can review my notes and assignments. (in order to)
   ____

C Editing **Circle the correct option to complete the sentences. In some sentences, both options are correct.**

I have not always thought carefully about my life choices, **so / so that** I have made some bad decisions in the past. However, I have tried to learn from my mistakes **so / so that** I can make better choices in future. For example, everyone told me I should be a lawyer, **so / so that** I went to law school. I soon realized that being a lawyer was not in fact what *I* wanted to do, **so / so that** I left after three months in order to study art. It was an important lesson, and it taught me that I should make decisions **so / so that** *I* am happy – not other people!

D **Plan and write your essay to answer the essay question. Then check your essay for errors.**

Listening extra *A passion for fashion*

A In your opinion, what are the three most important skills and abilities that a fashion designer needs? Check (✓) the boxes. Can you think of other ideas?

He or she needs to . . .

- ☐ be able to work under pressure.
- ☐ have a talent for drawing and art.
- ☐ be capable of taking control and managing people.
- ☐ be disciplined.
- ☐ be adept at predicting fashion trends.
- ☐ have a capacity for understanding others.

B Listen to an interview with Maxine Rothman, a fashion designer. Match the people and organizations with what Maxine says about them. Write the letters a–e.

1. Maxine ____
2. Maxine's mother ____
3. The designer in Paris ____
4. The fashion industry ____
5. Maxine's company ____

a. is not always environmentally responsible.
b. lets Maxine promote her ideas.
c. designs clothes for the office.
d. designs clothes for weekends.
e. trains designers to be disciplined.

Maxine

C Listen again. Circle the correct option to complete the sentences.

1. As a child, Maxine was particularly interested in **dolls / clothes**.
2. She first learned to create designs **in a fashion house / at home**.
3. Her mother always **pushed / encouraged** her to become a fashion designer.
4. She started her company because she wanted to **have more control / make more money**.
5. She wants everyone to know about her **ethical / disciplined** way of making clothes.
6. Maxine's employees are paid **as much as / more than** workers in the fashion industry.
7. Maxine's company is **incredibly relaxed / environmentally responsible**.
8. The company makes clothes that people **can wear for a long time / throw away each season**.

About you

D Answer the questions with information that is true for you.

1. Do you think that you have any of the skills to be a fashion designer? If so, which ones?
____
2. Would you like to have a career as a fashion designer? Why or why not?
____
3. What is your opinion of ethical clothing?
____
4. Do you try to buy ethical clothing? Why or why not?
____

Now complete the *Unit 12 Progress chart* on page 101.

Progress charts

Unit 1 Progress chart	
Mark the boxes to rate your progress. ☑ **I can do it.** ? **I can do it, but have questions.** ! **I need to review it.** I can . . .	To review, go back to these pages in the Student's Book.
☐ discuss friends, friendship, social networking, and compare networking habits.	12
☐ ask questions to get to know someone.	10
☐ use the present tense, *tend*, and *will* to talk about habits.	13
☐ describe people's personalities.	11
☐ ask questions to find out or check information.	14
☐ start questions with *And, But,* and *So* to link back to a previous speaker.	14
☐ use rising intonation to suggest answers to a question.	138
☐ write an argument using expressions like *whereas* to contrast ideas.	18

Unit 2 Progress chart	
Mark the boxes to rate your progress. ☑ **I can do it.** ? **I can do it, but have questions.** ! **I need to review it.** I can . . .	To review, go back to these pages in the Student's Book.
☐ describe and give opinions on the impact of the media and celebrities.	20
☐ use defining and non-defining relative clauses to give and add information.	21
☐ use *that* clauses to link ideas.	23
☐ choose the correct preposition after at least 12 key nouns.	22
☐ use *which* clauses to comment on my own and other people's statements.	21
☐ use *You know what . . . ?* to introduce a comment on what I'm going to say.	25
☐ use falling intonation in *which* clauses.	138
☐ use a topic sentence in a paragraph and expressions like *First* to list ideas.	28

Unit 3 Progress chart	
Mark the boxes to rate your progress. ☑ **I can do it.** ? **I can do it, but have questions.** ! **I need to review it.** I can . . .	To review, go back to these pages in the Student's Book.
☐ tell stories about my childhood, life experiences, and lessons learned.	34
☐ use the past tense and the present perfect to talk about the past.	31
☐ the simple past, past perfect, and past perfect continuous to sequence events.	33
☐ use at least 12 expressions to describe school-related experiences.	32
☐ interrupt a story I am telling to make a comment and then come back to it.	34
☐ use *(It's) no wonder* to say something is not surprising.	35
☐ reduce the auxiliary verbs *did* and *had.*	139
☐ write a narrative article using appropriate verb forms.	38

Unit 4 Progress chart

Mark the boxes to rate your progress. ☑ I can do it. ? I can do it, but have questions. ! I need to review it. I can . . .	To review, go back to these pages in the Student's Book.
☐ give advice on finding jobs and job interviews, and give opinions on benefits.	42
☐ identify and use countable and uncountable nouns correctly.	43
☐ use definite and indefinite articles to generalize and specify.	45
☐ use at least 12 verb + noun collocations on the topic of finding a job.	42
☐ use *-ly* adverbs to show my attitude toward what I say.	46
☐ use *As a matter of fact* or *In fact* to emphasize or correct information.	47
☐ stress the correct syllables in at least 15 words to talk about work.	139
☐ write a personal statement for an application using nouns instead of *I* + verb.	50

Unit 5 Progress chart

Mark the boxes to rate your progress. ☑ I can do it. ? I can do it, but have questions. ! I need to review it. I can . . .	To review, go back to these pages in the Student's Book.
☐ describe and give opinions on social problems, world issues and solutions.	54
☐ use conditional sentences to hypothesize about events in the present or past.	53
☐ use *wish* and *hope* to express wishes, hopes, and regrets.	55
☐ remember at least 12 words to talk about world problems and solutions.	54
☐ use *What if . . . ?, suppose,* and *imagine* to suggest possible scenarios or ideas.	56
☐ use *I suppose* to show that I'm not 100 percent sure.	57
☐ stress the correct syllables in different forms of 10 words for world issues.	140
☐ write an inquiry and use *it* as a subject or as an object.	60

Unit 6 Progress chart

Mark the boxes to rate your progress. ☑ I can do it. ? I can do it, but have questions. ! I need to review it. I can . . .	To review, go back to these pages in the Student's Book.
☐ talk about the future of money, technology, clothing, travel, and entertainment.	62
☐ use the present tense *be going to, will, might, may* to describe future events.	63
☐ use modal verbs for expectations, guesses, necessity, advice, requests, etc.	65
☐ remember at least 12 expressions to use when giving a presentation.	64
☐ use *would* or *'d* to soften my opinions.	66
☐ use *so* in responses like *I think so* to avoid repeating words.	67
☐ pronounce at least 12 words with silent consonants.	140
☐ structure a paragraph and use modal verbs with adverbs, like *will eventually*.	70

Progress charts

Unit 7 Progress chart	
Mark the boxes to rate your progress. ☑ **I can do it.** ? **I can do it, but have questions.** ! **I need to review it.** I can . . .	To review, go back to these pages in the Student's Book.
☐ discuss issues in getting along with people and experiences of growing up.	74
☐ use at least 12 phrasal verbs to discuss house rules and roommates.	75
☐ use infinitives and *-ing* forms to describe experiences.	77
☐ use expressions like *What I'm saying is* and *I mean* to make my meaning clear.	78
☐ use expressions like *I have to say* to show that I want to make a strong point.	79
☐ say at least six conversational expressions quickly.	141
☐ write a thesis statement using *What* clauses to introduce key points.	82

Unit 8 Progress chart	
Mark the boxes to rate your progress. ☑ **I can do it.** ? **I can do it, but have questions.** ! **I need to review it.** I can . . .	To review, go back to these pages in the Student's Book.
☐ discuss farming, food, nutrition, and a healthy diet.	84, 86
☐ use the passive to talk about the past, present and future.	85
☐ use complements of at least 10 verbs that describe causes and effects.	87
☐ name at least 12 human body parts and processes.	86
☐ use rhetorical questions to make a point.	88
☐ use *such as, like, take*, and *for instance* to give examples.	89
☐ decide when to say strong or weak forms of prepositions.	141
☐ write about graphs and charts, and use prepositions and approximate numbers.	92

Unit 9 Progress chart	
Mark the boxes to rate your progress. ☑ **I can do it.** ? **I can do it, but have questions.** ! **I need to review it.** I can . . .	To review, go back to these pages in the Student's Book.
☐ define and discuss success and happiness and share stories.	94
☐ use the determiners *all, both, each, every, neither none of, no.*	95
☐ use *-ing* forms as reduced relative clauses, for events and as subjects and objects.	97
☐ remember at least 10 expressions with *get.*	94
☐ use expressions like *As far as (success) is concerned* to focus in on a topic.	98
☐ use expressions like *As far as I'm concerned / can tell* to give and soften opinions.	99
☐ use appropriate stress in conversational expressions.	142
☐ write a paragraph in an essay using expressions like *in addition to*, to add ideas.	102

Unit 10 Progress chart

Mark the boxes to rate your progress. ☑ **I can do it.** ? **I can do it, but have questions.** ! **I need to review it.** I can . . .	To review, go back to these pages in the Student's Book.
☐ describe travel and vacations and discuss the effects of tourism.	106
☐ use at least 12 adjectives ending *-ed* and *-ing* to describe travel experiences.	106
☐ use reported speech to report statements, questions and instructions.	107, 109
☐ use expressions like *so what you're saying is* when drawing conclusions.	110
☐ say *In what way?* to ask for more details about someone's ideas or opinions.	111
☐ say at least 10 words which have silent or reduced vowels.	142
☐ write a survey article and use expressions like *although* to connect clauses.	114

Unit 11 Progress chart

Mark the boxes to rate your progress. ☑ **I can do it.** ? **I can do it, but have questions.** ! **I need to review it.** I can . . .	To review, go back to these pages in the Student's Book.
☐ talk about weddings, gifts, and traditions and discuss aspects of globalization.	116, 118
☐ use relative clauses with *when, where,* and *whose.*	117
☐ use verbs with two objects to describe giving things to people.	119
☐ remember at least 15 expressions to describe wedding customs.	116
☐ use expressions like *kind of, a little,* and *not really* to soften my comments.	120
☐ use *Yeah, no.* to agree with someone and then make a comment of my own.	121
☐ say consonant groups when one consonant is not pronounced.	143
☐ write a conclusion to an essay and explain cause and effect with *due to*, etc.	124

Unit 12 Progress chart

Mark the boxes to rate your progress. ☑ **I can do it.** ? **I can do it, but have questions.** ! **I need to review it.** I can . . .	To review, go back to these pages in the Student's Book.
☐ talk about intelligence, skills and abilities and how to develop talents.	126
☐ use adverbs before adjectives to introduce degree, type, opinion, and focus.	127
☐ use *as . . . as* and comparative and superlative adjectives and adverbs.	129
☐ use at least 12 expressions to describe types of intelligence and abilities.	126
☐ use vague expressions like *and all that* when I don't need to be precise.	130
☐ use *No doubt* to show that I strongly agree with someone.	131
☐ use appropriate stress and intonation for new information.	143
☐ write an essay and use expressions like *so that* to explain purpose.	134

Photography credits

2 Paul Bradbury/age fotostock
5 Suprijono Suharjoto/iStockphoto
6 *(woman)* age fotostock/SuperStock; *(background)* Neliyana Kostadinova/Shutterstock
8 Jared DeCinque/iStockphoto
9 *(left to right)* ostill/Shutterstock; Hongqi Zhang/iStockphoto; Justin Horrocks/iStockphoto; Supri Suharjoto/Shutterstock
11 Oleksiy Mark/Shutterstock
12 Andrea Danti/Shutterstock
14 CHASSENET/age fotostock
16 *(skateboarder)* Vladimir Ivanovich Danilov/Shutterstock; *(computer monitor)* Iakov Filimonov/Shutterstock; *(sample website)* Michael Monahan/Shutterstock
17 *(left to right)* Netfalls/Shutterstock; Rich Legg/iStockphoto; Jupiterimages/Thinkstock
19 Andy Cook/iStockphoto
21 Imagesource/Glow Images
22 *(boy)* Matthew Plexman/age fotostock; *(man)* Duncan Walker/iStockphoto; *(lion)* Kennan Ward/Corbis/Glow Images
24 Kuttig - Travel/Alamy
25 *(left to right)* Richard Semik/Shutterstock; ixer/Shutterstock; vilax/Shutterstock; Dima367/Dreamstime.com; IBI/Shutterstock
26 Dmitriy Shironosov/Shutterstock
28 Tom Mc Nemar/Shutterstock
33 Wavebreakmedia Ltd/Dreamstime
34 Gus Ruelas/AP Images
35 Jim West/Alamy
38 Claudia Dewald/iStockphoto
41 ©zhang bo/iStockphoto
42 Leslie Richard Jacobs/Corbis/Glow Images
43 *(woman)* Fancy/Veer/Corbis/Glow Images; *(globe)* Vasiliy Yakobchuk/iStockphoto
49 *(left to right)* Mlenny Photography/iStockphoto; Dawn Nichols/iStockphoto; Dmitry Skalev/iStockphoto; sculpies/iStockphoto
51 Brian Jackson/iStockphoto
52 Rosemarie Gearhart/iStockphoto
53 Andreas Kindler/Getty Images
54 *(top)* konstantynov/Shutterstock; *(bottom)* Pixtal/SuperStock
57 Tsian/Shutterstock
58 Seesea/Dreamstime.com
59 *(top)* Dorling Kindersley/Getty Images; *(bottom)* 4x6/iStockphoto
60 Yuri Arcurs/Shutterstock
61 drbimages/iStockphoto
62 Jim Jurica/iStockphoto
65 *(blueberries)* Stefanie Mohr Photography/Shutterstock; *(avocado)* Oliver Hoffmann/Shutterstock; *(cup of coffee)* Alexander Gatsenko/iStockphoto; *(fish)* Alexander Raths/Shutterstock
66 David Waldorf
68 *(top)* Justin Horrocks/iStockphoto; *(middle)* PT Images/Shutterstock; *(bottom)* Rido/Shutterstock
70 Jupiterimages/Getty Images
71 Özgür Donmaz/iStockphoto
73 Radius Images/Alamy
74 *(snake)* Colette3/Shutterstock; *(fish)* Raulin/Dreamstime.com
75 *(top)* Jacom Stephens/iStockphoto; *(left)* Jtinjaca/Dreamstime.com
76 Abel Mitja Varela/iStockphoto
78 *(books)* mattjeacock/iStockphoto; *(background)* Tamakiik/Shutterstock
81 *(forest)* Tul R./Shutterstock; *(monkey)* Eric Gevaert/iStockphoto
85 Jupiterimages, Brand X Pictures/Thinkstock
86 hugolacasse/Shutterstock
87 Rubberball/iStockphoto
89 *(top)* Johannes Compaan/iStockphoto; *(bottom)* Caroline von Tuempling/Getty Images
91 *(top)* Nick Free/iStockphoto; *(blog)* file404/Shutterstock
93 Stephan Bock/iStockphoto
94 *(top)* Allstar Picture Library/Alamy; *(middle)* FilmMagic/Getty Images; *(bottom)* FilmMagic/Getty Images; *(filmstrip)* Cowpland/Shutterstock
97 Diana Hirsch/iStockphoto

Text credits

Every effort has been made to trace the owners of copyrighted material in this book. We would be grateful to hear from anyone who recognizes his or her copyrighted material and who is unacknowledged. We will be pleased to make the necessary corrections in future editions of the book.

Corpus

Development of this publication has made use of the Cambridge English Corpus (CEC). The CEC is a computer database of contemporary spoken and written English, which currently stands at over one billion words. It includes British English, American English and other varieties of English. It also includes the Cambridge Learner Corpus, developed in collaboration with the University of Cambridge ESOL Examinations. Cambridge University Press has built up the CEC to provide evidence about language use that helps to produce better language teaching materials.